Computer Capacity Planning

Computer Capacity Planning
Theory and Practice

Shui F. Lam

Department of Mathematics and Computer Science
California State University
Long Beach, California

K. Hung Chan

Graduate School of Management
University of California, Riverside
Riverside, California

ACADEMIC PRESS, INC.
Harcourt Brace Jovanovich, Publishers

Boston Orlando San Diego
New York Austin London Sydney
Tokyo Toronto

Academic Press, Inc.
Orlando, Florida 32887

United Kingdom Edition published by
ACADEMIC PRESS INC. (LONDON) LTD.
24-28 Oval Road, London NW1 7DX

Library of Congress Cataloging-in-Publication Data

Lam, Shui F.
  Computer capacity planning.

  Bibliography: p.
  Includes index
  1. Computer capacity—Planning.   I. Chan, K. Hung.
II. Title.
QA76.9.C63L36   1987   004.2'1   86-32220
ISBN 0-12-434430-5 (alk. paper)

87 88 89 90   9 8 7 6 5 4 3 2 1
Printed in the United States of America

**To our Parents, and
Jo May and Jo Kay**

ACKNOWLEDGMENTS

The authors wish to express appreciation to the many colleagues and professional acquaintances who have made helpful comments on this monograph. We are especially indebted to James Pick of the University of California, Riverside, Art Gittleman of the California State University, Long Beach, Ronald Reed and William Denton of Home Savings of America for their detailed reviews and insightful suggestions for improvements. We have also received invaluable assistance and ideas from Tsung-Jen Chiu, Apichart Karoonkornsakul, HeeKyung Sung, and Christina K.Y. Yau.

An important element in the execution and completion of research project of this kind is the environment in which the effort took place. We thank Karl Anatol and Charles Austin of the California State University, Long Beach and Stepan Karamardian of the University of California, Riverside for their roles in providing this environment. Finally, to those hundreds of individuals who responded to our questionnaire survey, we are particularly grateful. We hope that the results of this research will be helpful to the survey respondents and others in the field of computer capacity planning.

Any shortcomings of this manuscript are the responsibility of the authors.

January 1987

Shui F. Lam

K. Hung Chan

COMPUTER CAPACITY PLANNING : THEORY AND PRACTICE

TABLE OF CONTENTS

COMPUTER CAPACITY PLANNING - THEORY AND PRACTICE

PREFACE

Increased computerization in business data processing has led to greater reliance on computers in business operations and growing data processing budgets. Many computer-related matters have become major management concerns. Satisfactory computer services depend greatly on the choice of configurations and the amount of capacity available on the computer system. To monitor and project computer workload and to plan for changes or expansions of computer configurations to meet future demand in a cost-effective manner is generally referred to as computer capacity planning. Because upgrading computer facilities often involves a large sum of money, improvements in capacity planning can mean substantial cost savings to the company.

This study examines the theory and practices of computer capacity planning in a more rigorous manner than previous studies. The first part of this study summarizes and discusses the theories and techniques presented in recent literature on computer capacity planning. The second part focuses on examining the degree of applicability of the theories and techniques and how different organizations may adopt different capacity planning methods.   It also identifies ways to improve the applicability of the theory and the quality of the practice on computer capacity planning.   A questionnaire was used to collect the necessary empirical evidences for this study.

The approach taken in this monograph should make it a useful reference for a wide range of readers.   Instead of using a "cookbook" style showing simply how to do capacity planning, we emphasize on assessing the usefulness of the various approaches and techniques in capacity planning.   The information provided in this monograph should be of interest to analysts and managers who are faced with the practical reality of computer capacity planning.   It should broaden their understanding of this function by knowing how other companies carry out this function and what techniques are available in the literature that can be used to improve results. As management advisers, internal and external auditors as well as other quality assurance personnel should also obtain insight on how to measure, evaluate, and improve performance of their own or their clients' computer facilities.   Equipment manufacturers and software developers should find the results of this study useful as they provide direct consumer information that will help guide the development of their new machines or new software packages.   An essential way to assess consumer behaviors is to contact the consumers directly.   As far as we can ascertain, this is the first study on computer capacity planning that directly solicits and analyzes a wide range of consumer information in a systematic and scientific manner.

Researchers may use the survey results to assess the future direction of research in computer capacity planning as these results provide insight into the degree of applicability of the various techniques under different business environments.   Finally, for students in computer science, information management and accounting/auditing, we offer a concise description of the principles of computer capacity planning.   The data and analysis of the practices enable students to better appreciate the usefulness of the capacity planning techniques in different circumstances.

LIST OF FIGURES

LIST OF TABLES

CHAPTER 1

ISSUES AND OVERVIEW

1.1 The Significance of Computer Capacity Planning

Electronic computing is a relatively new industry. In a history of thirty some years, electronic data processing has been ingrained into many aspects of people's daily life and certainly has established a strong foothold in business and non-business organizations. With more and more data stored electronically, more operations under computer guidance or control, and more users relying on computers to carry out their functions, it is inconceivable for many companies to be able to continue normal operations without the computer. The availability, reliability, serviceability, ease of use, rate of response, and other computer related matters have become major management concerns. As more operations are being computerized and more users are gaining access to the computer through their terminals, computer functions are very visible and computer performance is under close scrutiny. Data process- ing departments are often expected to provide satisfactory services in the most cost-effective manner.

Satisfactory computer services imply, among other things, high availability and reliability of the services, as well as adequate response time and turnaround time. All of these variables are in turn dependent on the choice of configurations including the amount of capacity available. To monitor and project computer workload and to plan for changing or expanding computer configurations to satisfy the future demand in a cost-effective manner is generally referred to as computer capacity planning. The term capacity here refers to the capacity of the system, not just that of the CPU. The term computer workload may have different meaning for different computer installations. Detailed discussion of this term will be given in Chapter 2. At this point we simply adopt an intuitive meaning of the term as the amount of work performed on the computer in a given period of time.

Computer capacity planning and computer performance management are closely related functions for the support of a computer installation. Performance management can be loosely defined as the monitoring and reporting of performance of the computer systems within the computer center's jurisdiction, and the identification and provision of corrective actions required to maintain the performance at an acceptable level. As will be apparent in Chapters 2 and 3, measuring and evaluating performance are necessary for proper planning of computer capacity expansion and upgrade. For discussions in this monograph, therefore, computer capacity planning encompasses many aspects of performance management.

Kelly [1983] cited in his report the following reasons for conducting capacity planning:

. DP budgets are significant in proportion to the total budget in most large corporations.

. Corporate profits and organizational efficiency are becoming increasingly dependent upon computer performance.

. With the increased use of terminal-driven systems, computer performance is visible to a much wider audience than it has been in the past.

. Computer systems are becoming so complex and diverse that control is difficult to maintain.

In order to satisfy user demands for more computing power, in order to use the most up-to-date technology to increase computer availability and reliabililty, and in order to provide "easier to use" computer facilities, data processing departments across the nation must constantly monitor what is available in the market and try to acquire the most suitable facilities within the budget allowed. The amount of acquisition is evident from the sales statistics as shown in Table 1.1.

From Table 1.1, the total sales of the ten major computer companies show an increase of 9% in 1985 and 16% in 1984. These increases are especially significant when compared to the moderate average increase in sales of 2.75% and 4.27% respectively for 1985 and 1984 for the Fortune 500 industrial companies [Fortune 1984, 1985, 1986].

The need for the planning of expansion of computer facilities exists in all computer installations, but is especially important in org-

TABLE 1.1

INCREASE IN SALES OF THE TEN LARGEST COMPUTER COMPANIES*

Company	1985 Sales	1984 Sales	1983 Sales	% Increase 84 to 85	% Increase 83 to 84
IBM	50,056	45,937	40,180	9	14
Digital Equipment	6,686	5,584	4,272	20	31
Honeywell	6,625	6,138	5,753	8	7
Hewlett Packard	6,505	6,044	4,710	8	28
Sperry	5,687	5,238	5,076	9	3
Burroughs	5,038	4,808	4,296	5	12
NCR	4,317	4,074	3,731	6	9
Wang	2,352	2,185	1,538	8	42
Apple	1,918	1,516	983	27	54
Data General	1,239	1,161	829	7	40
Total	90,423	82,685	71,368		
Overall increase in percentage				9	16

* Ranking based on Fortune 500 industrial firms listed according to 1985 sales in million dollars. Control Data Corp. was not included due to the unavailability of comparable data as a result of accounting changes in 1985.

Sources: The Fortune 500, 1984, 1985, and 1986.

anizations with mainframe or large minicomputers. To obtain additional computer capacity or new equipment in a mainframe or large minicomputer installation usually involves a large sum of money. For example, an IBM 3081 processor or a Sperry 1100/90 series processor costs at least several million dollars, and most large minicomputer processors are priced at hundreds of thousand dollars [Henkel, 1983]. In view of the need for frequent acquisitions and the large amount of resources involved, even a slight improvement on computer capacity planning can amount to sizable savings. Discussions in this book will therefore focus on computer capacity planning methodologies for mainframe and minicomputer installations, although many of the ideas and principles included in these methodologies are also applicable to the planning of microcomputers.

1.2 The Capacity Planning Process

Due to the amount of resources involved, all major configuration changes in mainframe and large minicomputer installations require the approval from upper-level management and must be carefully planned for. Computer configuration changes are often due to the occurrence of many interrelated events. A primary reason for equipment upgrades is that the existing configuration is no longer adequate to support the current or expected future workload generated by existing as well as new applications. Other reasons may include: change of users and/or user requirements, the need for software updates, expiration of equipment

lease, and technological advances.   Therefore, computer capacity planning should be an on-going and reiterative process incorporating all
these pertinent factors into consideration to anticipate changes to ensure their orderly implementation.   This planning process may include
the following basic steps:

- Knowing what equipment (purchased, leased, or rented) and how much
  capacity we have now.
- Knowing how much workload is being processed today and the characteristics (include seasonal patterns) of this workload regarding
  its resource consumption.
- Setting performance objectives for the computer facilities considering costs, quality of services, technological developments,
  etc.
- Forecasting the rate of growth of the existing workload and the
  amount of new workload to be installed within the planning horizon
  (Growth rate beyond upgrade point is also required for the analysis
  of alternatives).
- Identifying the time when the increasing workload will exceed the
  current capacity or performance threshold.

After this process, we can then investigate alternatives and
request approval of acquiring the new capacity at the required time.   In
companies which have business systems planning or other similar planning
process implemented [Zachman 1982, King 1978], a computer capacity plan
should be analyzed within its context.   Business systems planning attempts to identify enterprise-wide opportunities for employing informa-

tion technologies, prioritize these various opportunities, and establish an enterprise-level architecture from the perspective of long-term benefits to the business unit as a whole. Therefore, alternatives for system changes to alleviate capacity shortage problems identified from a capacity study can be compared within the enterprise-wide priority structure and the enterprise-level architecture. Trade-offs between long-term and short-term options can then be made in the capacity upgrade decisions for the overall interest of the business at a given point in time.

1.3 Objectives of the Monograph

A traditional capacity planning method measures the utilization of each major component in the computer system (e.g., CPU, memory, I/O channels, disk, printers, etc.). Some rule-of-thumb utilization thresholds are established for each component (e.g., 35% for I/O channel, 75% for CPU, etc.). When the measured utilization for a component exceeds its corresponding utilization threshold, a bottleneck is expected to exist and something should be done to remove it -- usually by shifting workload, modifying software, or upgrading capacity.

There are many more sophisticated techniques proposed in the published literature for carrying out the function of capacity planning including those used for projecting workload and predicting capacity shortage. Different amounts of effort and details are required for the various techniques resulting in different degrees of accuracy. Application of these techniques can be found in some computer installations, but their extensive use is not common. Many companies still rely on the simplistic, rules-of-thumb, or judgmental approach. (On many occasions, they do find the results acceptable.) There appears to be a significant gap between theory and practice as to the usability of the scientific and the more sophisticated techniques in this vital function of computer capacity planning which, if done properly, may save millions of dollars for the organization. This research study outlines the state of the art in computer capacity planning, discusses the techniques proposed in recent literature, ascertains and evaluates the methods being actually applied in practice under different business and computing environments, assesses the gap between theory and practice, and recommends ways to bridge this gap for the benefits of both theorists and practitioners in the field. Thus, this study should be of interest to researchers, data processing managers and analysts including those in charge of computer capacity planning and performance evaluation, auditors and quality assurance personnels, equipment manufacturers, software developers, as well as students in information sciences.

1.4 Literature Review

Most textbooks on data center operations and management have devoted one of more chapters on the principles of computer capacity planning to discuss issues like capacity measurement, performance evaluation, workload forecasting, as well as the financial aspects of hardware acquisition such as purchase versus lease decisions, charging for computer services, etc. Recent publications in this area include Schaeffer [1981], Strauss [1981], Axelrod [1982], Cortada [1983], and Borovits [1984]. These authors have unanimously stressed the importance of computer capacity planning in managing data centers.

Even more texts are written on the theories of performance evaluation emphasizing on the techniques and tools developed recently in this area. Examples include Kleinrock [1975, 1976], Ferrari and Spadoni (ed.) [1981], Law and Kelton [1981], Morris and Roth [1982], Ferrari, Serazzi and Zeigner [1983], Lavenberg (ed.) [1983], and Lazowska, et al. [1984]. These books present the various tools and techniques developed for computer performance measurement and evaluation. These include hardware and software monitors, benchmarking, simulation, analytic models, and software physics. Large quantities of professional and academic papers have also been published in this area, reporting advances in new tools and techniques, as well as some personal experiences on projects applying the various tools developed in house or externally. Many notable publications can be found in the references, for examples, Denning and Buzen [1978], Buzen [1980], Chandy and Neuse [1982], Sauer and MacNair [1982], Jalswal [1983], Barkataki [1984], Brumfield [1984], Anderson [1984], Lewis et al. [1985], and Stroebel et al. [1986].

While much of the published literature has concentrated on explaining the principles and techniques of computer capacity planning, not much work has been done to assess the extent these principles and techniques are being applied in practice. A major exception is the report by Kelly [1983]. The report reviewed the practice based on interviews with industry and government leaders, and the personal experience of the author. It presented a summary of opinions expressed by the interviewees on the various issues about computer capacity planning, including the definition of capacity, capacity measurement, and planning tools used. However, the report does not disclose the number of interviewees and how the sample was selected. No statistics were given as to what techniques were being applied under what circumstances and the extent of their application. Morino Associates [1983] provides another report on capacity planning practices. The survey was conducted in 1982. Unlike our study, their survey focused primarily on an evaluation of the usage of software packages for performance management and capacity planning by IBM MVS (Multiple Virtual System) users.

It is felt that a more rigorous methodology using a more systematic and scientific approach and a sample representing a wider spectrum of users is necessary to better assess the usefulness in the real world of the various tools of computer capacity planning under different circumstances. This research study is intended to fill this gap in the literature. Futhermore, our study provides more up-to-date information on this aspect of computer management in a rapidly changing technological environment.

1.5 Organization of the Monograph

In the five chapters that follow, we will present the theory as well as the practices in computer capacity planning. Chapter 2 introduces the major elements in the process of computer capacity planning. An explanation on the functions of each element and the various techniques and tools for carrying out these functions will be presented. In Chapter 3 we will show how these elements can be tied together to achieve the objective of computer capacity planning; that is, matching computer resources to computer workload in a cost-effective manner.

These two chapters will provide a concise summary of the fundamental concepts of computer capacity planning, as well as an evaluation of the various approaches and techniques that are available for the implementation of the planning process. For the readers who wish to understand the essential ingredients of the computer capacity planning process, and for those who are currently in charge of the capacity planning function and who are looking for new methods for improvement, these two chapters should provide valuable information. Those who already have a good understanding of the process and are primarily interested in gaining a better appreciation of industry practices may go directly to Chapters 4, 5, and 6. Such an appreciation often helps capacity planners identify where their own installations stand relative to other companies in terms of the application of the various advance methodologies, which can be useful in assessing the need for changes.

The empirical study on computer capacity planning practices will be first introduced in Chapter 4. The survey methodology including the questionnaire, its distributions and responses will be discussed. The overall results of the survey, based on the questionnaire responses, will be presented and analyzed. Chapter 5 focuses on how environmental characteristics may affect the practices of capacity planning based on the survey results.   Where applicable, statistical tests will be used to enhance the analyses of our survey data.

Chapter 6 identifies a number of significant differences between theory and practices in computer capacity planning.   It also recommends some measures to improve the theory and practice of computer capacity planning.

CHAPTER 2

THE TASKS IN COMPUTER CAPACITY PLANNING

2.1 Introduction

A cost-effective program for the monitoring and projection of computer workload and the planning for the changes and acquisitions of
computer facilities to satisfy the projected future demand relies on a
systematic methodology to handle the tasks involved. The first task in
the process is to prepare an inventory of the computer installation.
Other tasks include the determination of workload measures and workload
characteristics, the evaluation and selection of performance indexes,
monitoring and measuring workload and performance, workload forecasting,
setting capacity limits and performance objectives as well as performance predictions. Based on the experience of the authors and others,
this chapter will describe the nature of these tasks in some detail as
well as the implementation issues related to these tasks. A discussion
of the various techniques that one can employ to carry out these tasks
and an assessment of these techniques will also be provided.

2.2   Inventory

A prerequisite of an effective computer capacity planning process is a comprehensive inventory of the existing computer installation. This inventory should include the hardware, system software, and applications software components whether they are purchased, leased, rented, or licensed. Such an inventory will provide a "here and now" picture of the installation from which future changes to the installation can be planned and impact can be adequately assessed before a change is implemented.

The inventory needs to be periodically reviewed and updated. During the review, equipment with expiring lease (say, in six months), software with new releases offering substantially different features, and hardware components with new models giving significantly improved price/performance advantages and features should be noted. Noting of such events should trigger the initiation of a specific capacity study which may result in a plan for configuration change. The inventory can be computerized. For example, a database can be used to record all the inventory items with their attributes (class of item such as hardware, system or application software; ownership type such as purchased, leased, rented, or licenced; lease expiration date if applicable; is the item sharable or dedicated to a particular processor; processor to which the item is dedicated; physical location of hardware items; and so on). With a comprehensive inventory database, data can be retrieved by specifying the desired attribute value. For instance, a list of hardware located at the head office with lease expiring within the next six months can easily be printed.

2.2.1 Hardware Inventory

The hardware inventory should include all hardware components, e.g., processors, memory modules, disk controllers, disk pack units, tape drives, local and remote terminals, communications controllers, switching units, multiplexers, etc. Other information should also be kept in the inventory records including configuration diagrams showing how these units are interconnected, model number of each component, pertinent characteristics of each component and the interconnecting cables. For example, for the CPU, we should identify the CPU model number, processor speed, the memory capacity and cycle time, the models that can be upgraded to and their capability/capacity, order lead time for upgrades, how the CPU is configured (e.g., whether the dual processors are configured as tightly coupled or loosely coupled processing units, what peripherals and how many of them are directly controlled by the CPU), cost of the CPU, financing arrangements (e.g., purchased or leased or rented, lease expiration date), cost of maintenance and insurance, when the CPU was installed, expected life cycle, what backup possibilities are available in case of severe failure, and so on.

2.2.2 System Software Inventory

The inventory for system software includes the operating systems, all the language processors (e.g., FORTRAN, COBOL, APL, etc.), the time-sharing control system (e.g., TSO, CMS, UNIX, etc.), the online application control system (e.g., CICS on IBM, TIPS on UNIVAC), database management system (e.g., IMS on IBM, DBMS on VAX), and other relevant facilities.   It may be argued, for instance, whether the FORTRAN compiler should be counted as a system or application software.   From the operating system's standpoint, a FORTRAN compiler or a database management system (DBMS) such as IMS is executed at the same level as any other application programs in the system.   However, from the user's standpoint, a FORTRAN compiler or a DBMS is part of the computing environment in which his or her application programs are to run. Moreover, these software systems are installed for all users and their ownership is often more appropriate that of the data center.   In addition, the data center will have the responsibility to keep these software systems up-to-date.   For these reasons, it is important for the data center to maintain a detailed inventory of these software packages keeping track of such data as the version and level, contract period, cost, hardware environment required, resource requirements, limitations (if any), vendors, vendor supports, and alternatives.

2.2.3 Application Software Inventory

Application software can be grouped into two large categories: those large applications such as payroll and customer billings that have regular production run schedules (e.g., every month end), and those user programs which are submitted for execution by the user as needs arise. Due to their regularity, resource requirements for applications of the production-type can be monitored and relationships between resource requirements and external factors such as business volume can be identified. (See, for example, Sarna [1979].) Such relationships can be useful in two ways. First, they can be used to develop forecasts of future workload due to this category of applications given forecasts of the external factors. Second, most of these applications software packages are large and many are critical to the company's operations. Therefore adequate resources must be available to ensure their execution on time. As Umbaugh [1982] suggested, a list of the critical applications in order of decreasing priorities can be established with resource requirements identified for each so that a configuration for contingency can be planned that will allow the critical applications to run during a disaster situation. The configuration for contingency can be implemented by installing the additional computer resources as identified in a separate site, or acquiring agreement from a computer service bureau to provide the required configuration in case of a disaster.

The second category of applications (programs which normally belong to individual users and do not have regular run schedules) have become prominent with the popularity of terminals allowing much easier and direct access by users to the computer. These are called the demand-type applications. As need arises, a user logs in at a terminal and generates workload to the computer by using some commercial software packages, running some programs specifically developed for him, or even developing his or her own programs. This type of workload does not have any definite schedule, and the volume is often irregular. However, they usually appear during day time working hours (e.g., 8 a.m. - 5 p.m.) and peaks for a few hours each day. Users of these applications generally either work in interactive mode or submit and wait for batch program output at the terminal (referred to as demand batch). Most installations have a large number of these users. Performance of the system in terms of interactive response time and batch turnaround time becomes a sensitive issue to this group of users as well as data processing management. Capacity planning of most computer installations today is actually driven by this group of application users. (See, for example, Emrick [1984] and Schindler [1984].) An inventory of these application programs will be too large and not stable enough to be of much use. The workload due to these application programs may be ascertained through better understanding of the users involved. Hence, for demand-type applications, a current list of users from each department, categorized by the type of terminals used (local or remote) and the most frequently used set of applications (e.g., APL, SAS, database inquiry, financial software package, etc.) will be a more useful inventory for the purpose of capacity planning.

2.3   Workload Measures and Workload Characterizations

2.3.1   Hardware-Oriented Workload Measures

In order to monitor workload growth and to project the future demand, the unit of workload must be defined. Traditionally, workload is measured in units that describe hardware resource consumption such as CPU hours, I/O counts, disk space allocated, and lines or pages printed.

The use of these units implies that each hardware resource is measured separately and the workload is closely related to the utilization of the hardware component being measured.   Future workload projected in terms of these measures can readily be translated into future resource requirements.

Some vendors have proposed composite measures such as IBM's service unit, UNIVAC's standard unit of processing, and Boeing Computer Service's computer resource unit.   These are basically some weighted sums of the usage of the major resources including the CPU, memory and I/O.   The operating system uses these composite quantities for the scheduling of resource allocation among competing jobs.   The problem with their use in capacity planning lies with the difficulty in establishing an upper bound for the capacity of a given computer system in terms of these composite units.   However, measuring workload in these units can readily show the overall workload trend using one index.

2.3.2   User-Oriented Workload Measures

An important aspect of capacity planning is the forecasting of workload which should logically be related to the company's economic forecasts, business plans as well as each user department's specific plans.   However, workload measured in terms of hardware resource consumption bears no direct correspondence with business quantities such as sales and personnel level.   Some users find it difficult to make reliable forecasts of their department's computer workload in terms of CPU hours, I/O counts, etc.   For these reasons, it often becomes necessary to adopt some user-oriented measures in defining computer workload.

For the production-type applications such as payroll, relationship may be found between hardware resource consumption and some business measures such as the number of payroll records. For example, Sarna [1979] used regression to relate CPU and I/O utilizations in an accounts receivable application with three key volume indicators (user-oriented measures): number of invoices, number of updates, and number of open-term records. Estimates based on these relationships and values of the key volume indicators were found to be satisfactory. With proper relationships established through techniques such as regression analysis, forecasts in the user-oriented measures can be mapped into hardware-oriented workload. This approach of workload forecasting falls into the class of structural forecasting models which will be discussed later in this chapter.

For the demand-type applications, user-oriented workload measures may be related to the number of users, total amount of time spent at the terminal and the type of programs run. Every user department's demand-type workload may be measured by parameters of this kind which can then be mapped into hardware resource consumption based on user profiles data (to be described in the next subsection). Each user department when planning for future work programs will estimate the total personnel hours his or her staff will spend on computer-related projects, and the percent of time to be spent at the terminal can then be estimated based on past experience. With these projections from each user department, the data center can obtain hardware resource requirements projections for the demand-type applications. Adding demand-type projections to the production-type projections will provide a forecast for the workload growth due to existing applications.

User-oriented workload measures encourage meaningful user input into the workload forecasting process. These measures must be eventually mapped to the hardware resource requirements for the purpose of capacity planning. A substantial modeling effort will be required for an accurate mapping.

2.3.3 Workload Characterization

A quantitative description of the workload's characteristics is commonly known as the workload characterization. The description is usually given in terms of parameters that allow inference on resource utilization.

In general, workload characterization of the interactive workload may include the number of users simultaneously connected to the system, mean user think time (average time users spend between transactions), and the resource requirements for each transaction. For the batch workload, it may include the batch job arrival pattern, throughput rate, and each job's resource requirements. The description of resource requirements for each basic workload component (an interactive command or a batch job) may include CPU time, number of I/O operations, memory space, amount of input records and output lines, number of disk files accessed, number of tape units used, etc.

Due to the diversity of workload in most computer installations, the resource requirements of one workload component can be vastly different from another component. A workload characterization giving mean values for each parameter may bear no representation of the real workload. In this case, different and disjoint classes of workload should be defined each with a unique set of resource requirements and representing a portion of the total existing workload. Cluster analysis techniques [Anderberg 1973] may be used to achieve the classifications. The results are sometimes referred to as the application profiles.

Similar analysis can be applied to construct user profiles where the users (or a representative sample of users if the user population is large) will be grouped into disjoint classes. Each class can be characterized by parameters such as mean number of connect hours to the system per day, mean CPU time and number of I/O operations per connect hour, mean number of disk files accessed, percentage of interactive in total computer use, etc. In other words, user profiles define the resource consumption characteristics of the different groups of users in the organization.

The application profiles are useful in contingency planning as well as in workload forecast for new applications. As stated earlier, contingency planning requires the identification of critical applications and their resource requirements, thereby a sufficient configuration can be prepared to provide service during disaster situations. The application profiles therefore provide the necessary information for such a planning effort.

For the new applications that are under development or to be acquired, an estimate of the resource requirements is necessary. To obtain such an estimate, the application is first divided into parts or modules that perform complete functions. Resource requirements of each module are estimated either from the application profiles of existing modules with similar functions and structures, or based on an analysis of its structure, the operations involved, and its dependency on the input data. A good explanation on the latter approach can be found in [Ferrari et al. 1983, pp.124-142]. An estimate of the frequency that each module is executed allows us to estimate the overall resource requirements of the new application. The frequency of execution of each module can be estimated through an analysis of the number of users of the new application, the functions these users need to perform with the application, how often they need to perform these functions and a mapping of these functions to the modules in the application.

The resource consumption characteristics defined in the user profiles allow the mapping of the different classes of users into an estimate of resource requirements. Therefore the demand-type applications as described in the last section can be projected given a projection of the number of users in each user class. The total resource requirements projected for the existing production-type, the existing demand-type, and the new applications will account for the total future workload within the forecast horizon.

It should be noted that both the application and user profiles may change due to hardware or software changes in the system. For example, the use of personal computers in place of terminals to allow some computing to be performed locally on the personal computers, or a change from a line editor to a screen editor for text editing, can drastically affect the resource consumption patterns at the mainframe facilities.

Indeed, software packages with increasing size and sophistication are necessitated by user demands to do more on the computer with more ease (user-friendliness). This phenomenon has great impact on the computer resource comsumption pattern of individual users and applications, as well as the computer system as a whole. This effect should therefore be estimated before the hardware or software changes take place. The system modeling approach to be discussed in Chapter 3 can be applied to predict the effect.

2.4 Performance Indexes

From a data center's point of view, the computer system is installed to service the users in the organization. Therefore performance in this context should logically take the view of the users who are only interested in the processing of their programs. Several user-viewed performance indexes are commonly accepted: turnaround time, response time and availability. Data center management may also be interested in performance measures such as throughput and capacity when comparing among computer hardware of different models. System upgrade decisions should be related to the performance indexes that are significant to both the users and the data center management. It is therefore important to define and understand these performance indexes.

2.4.1 Turnaround Time

Turnaround time is defined as the time interval between the instant a program is read into the system for processing and the instant the program execution is completed. In modern systems, the program output is often temporarily stored on a disk unit from which the user can retrieve the output for viewing at a terminal. Subsequent printing of the output can result from a print command issued by the user. The times spent on viewing and the subsequent printing are not counted as part of the turnaround time of the original program submission.

Suppose N batch programs have been executed during a measurement period, and let T_i be the turnaround time of the ith job. Then the mean turnaround time T can be defined as:

$$T = \frac{\sum_{i=1}^{N} T_i}{N} \tag{2.1}$$

It should be noted that the mean turnaround time as defined above is dependent on the processing requirement of the jobs in the system under consideration. A system with a mean turnaround time of 20 minutes is not necessarily less efficient than one with a 10 minute turnaround. The longer turnaround is quite possibly due to the longer processing requirement of the jobs in that system. To normalize the difference in processing time requirements, a weighted turnaround time can be defined as the ratio between the turnaround time and the program's processing time, and the mean weighted turnaround time is defined as:

$$G = \frac{\sum\limits_{i=1}^{N} G_i}{N} \qquad\qquad (2.2)$$

Where G_i is the weighted turnaround time of the ith job executed during the measurement period.

2.4.2 Response Time

The equivalence of turnaround time in an interactive system is the response time. It is defined as the time interval from the instant a command inputs to the system (i.e., the moment when the user hits the enter key after typing the command) to the instant the corresponding reply begins to appear at the terminal. The internal response time refers to the time interval between the instant a command has reached the operating system and the instant the execution of the command is completed. The response time generally perceived by the user is the actual waiting for completing his or her command. It therefore includes the internal response time and the delay for transmitting the command and the system response in the communications network that links the terminal and the processor. The delay on the network includes the time the incoming command and the outgoing response spend on the front-end processor, the communication line, as well as the terminal controller.

Suppose that N commands have been recorded during a measurement period and R_i is the response time of the ith command, then the mean response time is defined as:

$$R = \frac{\displaystyle\sum_{i=1}^{N} R_i}{N} \qquad\qquad (2.3)$$

The variation in response time has been shown to have significant effect on user attitude which, in turn, affects productivity (see, for example, Miller [1976]). Therefore, measures such as the standard deviation and the percentiles which provide indication of the variability of the response time are useful supplementary indexes.

The standard deviation of response time is given by:

$$r = \sqrt{\frac{1}{N} \sum_{i=1}^{N} (R_i - R)^2} \qquad\qquad (2.4)$$

The pth percentile response time corresponds to the response time that is greater than p percent of all observed response time during a measurement period. Standard deviation is a useful measure of dispersion whereas percentiles can be more meaningful with asymmetric distributions of response time.

2.4.3 Availability

Availability is defined as the percentage of the total time during which the user has access to the system. The system becomes unavailable either due to scheduled preventive maintenance during operating hours, or unscheduled down time due to system failures, utility problems, etc. The system may be down due to hardware or software failures.

Availability is measured by the ratio of the time the system stays up and running and the total time the computer system is in operation. Low availability is a common cause for user dissatisfaction, especially during unscheduled down time. Also, reduced availability cuts into the amount of time for operation. This implies longer operating hours or earlier upgrade compared to an equivalent system with higher availability. Therefore equipment and software reliability and availability must be a major consideration in any evaluation of configuration alternatives.

2.4.4 Throughput

Throughput is generally considered as a measure of the system's productivity, therefore, it is of interest to the data center management. A generally recognized definition of throughput is N/L, where N is the number of programs or transactions processed during L, the measurement period.

The measured throughput is a function of the efficiency of the computer system as well as the workload. While there are jobs in backlog, then the faster the system, the more jobs can be finished. On a given system, as long as the system capacity has not been saturated, higher throughput is achieved with heavier workload. A comparison of throughput on two different systems is therefore meaningful only when they process the same batch of input jobs or there is an unlimited stream of input jobs of similar characteristics.

2.4.5 Capacity

The capacity of a system is the maximum amount of work the system is capable of doing per unit time. Ferrari [1983] differentiates between theoretical capacity and utilizable capacity. Theoretical capacity represents the maximum amount of work obtainable from the system. There are, however, constraints on a system's operation imposed by the workload's characteristics (e.g., I/O bound workload) and by the system's configuration (e.g., the number of communication lines and the type of terminals in the network). It is not uncommon for a resource to be capable of handling only a fraction of its theoretical capacity. The consideration of service objectives that specify, for example, average terminal response time in providing interactive services, further limits the maximum amount of work the system can handle. Therefore, it is the utilizable capacity that is of interest for capacity planning.

2.5 Workload and Performance Measurement

2.5.1 Data Collection and Analysis

To carry out the computer capacity planning function, a capacity planner must have adequate knowledge of the system's workload and performance. Such knowledge can be acquired through system monitoring where workload and performance data are collected and analyzed.

The workload and performance data may be collected on a continuous basis, i.e., all events regarding the computer workload and performance are detected and pertinent data recorded (full trace monitoring). Sampling may also be employed in data collection in order to reduce the overhead in processing as well as storage of data. When the event-driven method of monitoring is used, sampling means that observation is made in, say, every hundredth occurrence of the events of interest. When monitoring is time-driven, then activities are examined periodically at some fixed time intervals. In some cases, installations may not have an on-going process for the collection of workload and/or performance data. Instead, data are collected on an ad hoc basis when the need for analysis of the computer system or component in question arises.

The collected raw data allow system or component activities to be analyzed, workload pattern to be identified and characterized, and system or component performance to be measured and evaluated. When full trace monitoring is used, the analysis may use all data recorded during a selected measurement period. This approach tends to involve an exorbitant mass of data thus requiring a considerable amount of CPU time for the data collection and analysis. Under this circumstance, the desire to limit processing overhead may lead to the decision of using a shorter study period. Alternatively, sampling techniques may be adopted in the selection of data for analysis. For example, instead of analyzing the data of all days during the study period, randomly selected days may be used. The sampling technique employed must ensure that a representative subset of data is selected. If, for example, Thursday is known to be the busiest day in every week, then the sample selected must include sufficient number of Thursdays for analysis. Detailed discussions on the various sampling methods and their underlying assumptions can be found in the classic work of Cochran [1963].

2.5.2 Measurement Tools

Tools for measuring computer system activities can be grouped into three categories: hardware monitors, software monitors, and resource accounting monitors (See, for example, [Morris and Roth 1982]). Hardware monitors are electromechanical devices which may be connected to the computer system being measured with probes. They are capable of detecting change of signals which indicate activities that take place within that portion of the system being connected. The main characteristic of hardware monitors is that they are external to the system being measured. As a result, they do not use any of the system's resources during data collection, and do not cause any substantial overhead due to the measurement.

Software monitors are programs that supplement a system's operating system to collect information about the execution of one or more programs or about all or part of the hardware configuration. They may be either event-driven, time-driven, or a combination of both event-driven and time-driven. An event is said to have taken place in a hardware or software component of the system when a change of state occurs in that component. For example, when a processor stops executing instructions to await completion of an input or output sequence, we say that the processor changes from the "CPU busy" state to "CPU wait" state. The initiation or termination of a computer job will also con-

stitute an event to be recorded. Event-driven monitors collect information when the events of interest occur.   Each occurrence of these
events causes the processor to suspend temporarily what it is processing
at the moment to execute the software monitor code.   The suspended
program will be resumed when the monitor completes its execution. When
the events being measured occured too frequently, thus incurring excessive data and processing overhead, sampling may be employed by switching
to the monitor code, say, only every hundredth occurrence. An alternative method of data collection consists of detecting the states and
recording relevant data of individual system components at predetermined
time instants.   These tools are called time-driven monitors.   Time-
driven monitors sometimes are called samplers since, by their very
nature, they only observe a sample of the events that may occur.   The
overhead of time-driven monitors depends on the number of activities
measured at each sampling instant and the sampling frequency.

Most medium to large computer systems produce some form of resource
accounting data using accounting monitors.   The amount of data ranges
from simple logs of job or program submissions to comprehensive resource
usage accounting giving detailed data on overall use of the system's total capacity as well as breakdowns of resource usage of individual components by individual users and programs.   The SMF (System Management
Facility) [IBM 1977] on the IBM mainframe computers that run under the
MVS (Multiple Virtual Storage) operating system is an example of a comprehensive accounting monitor.   It collects information on the occurrence of system events such as the logon and logoff of terminal users,
individual job starts and terminations, opening and close of files, job

input and output statistics, and allocation of system resources to individual jobs. A great deal of the workload and performance data can be deduced from these comprehensive accounting data when they are available. Usually these resource accounting monitors allow options to be selected at system generation time so that the program collects only the data required. It is therefore necessary for capacity planners to get involved with the operations personnel for the selection of appropriate options in the installation of a resource accounting monitor package.

The major shortcomings of even the most comprehensive accounting monitor are (i) the lack of data collection capability on operating system activities, and (ii) the lack of data on the execution of portions within an application program. Software monitors are therefore necessary for the collection of these data. This is especially true in many installations where transaction processing is controlled by a single large application program. This large application is often started in the morning by the computer operations staff, remains active all day, and ends in the evening at a predetermined time again by the operations staff. The accounting monitor treats the application program as one entity and data collected is only relevant to the execution of the entire program. For performance evaluation and capacity planning purpose, the execution and resource requirement of individual transactions (each is handled by a module in the application program) are important information that cannot be obtained from the data collected by the accounting monitor. The CICS (Customer Information Control System) and IMS (Information Management System) on the IBM mainframe computers are typical examples of this type of application programs that require software monitors for collecting necessary workload and performance data.

2.6 Workload Forecasting

2.6.1 Problems in Workload Forecasting

The measurement of workload and performance on the current system allows us to determine the fraction of the system's capacity that has been utilized.   Workload increases will sooner or later saturate the system's capacity which, if left unresolved, will result in degraded performance.   Poor system performance reduces user productivity.   Some users may decide to use other means to solve problems which would normally be done on the computers.   To avoid capacity saturation, one must be able to predict the future workload.

Workload forecasting is typically the weakest element in the computer capacity planning process.   The first problem lies with the lack of a good definition of workload.   A common workload measure, CPU hours consumed, is too abstract for the user community, cannot be related easily to other business measures (e.g., sales, invoices) in the organization, and does not reflect workload to other components in the computer system.   Users therefore often feel unable to provide meaningful input to the workload forecast process.

Another problem relates to new applications.   The future workload due to existing applications is often forecasted based on historical data. Applications under development, applications to be acquired, significantly upgraded versions of existing applications, as well as applications newly in production, do not have historical data that one can base on to estimate their impact on the system's capacity. Lack of communication between the application development group and the capacity planning group can compound the problem even further. Estimates on workload due to new applications are typically wild guesses. Recently proposed methodologies try to correct this problem by integrating performance and capacity planning considerations into the application design [Friedman 1985, Lazowska et al. 1984, pp. 323-327].

The third problem in computer workload forecasting is due to the latent workload, that is, the portion of a workload that is not submitted to the system due to various reasons (e.g., poor system performance). The latent workload will reemerge in the future (e.g., when the system is upgraded or the performance problems are solved). Latent workload may also be hidden in the existing workload under a different form. For example, when the turnaround time of batch programs becomes too long, the users may use more often the online facilities. As soon as the batch performance improves, some portion of the online load may well revert back to batch to take advantage of the lower charge for the batch service. Latent workload is a largely unknown factor in the area of workload forecasting that requires more attention. At present, it can only be estimated by experience and through careful interviews with the various people involved (e.g., programmers, systems analysts, managers and heavy users).

Most common forecasting methods can be applied to forecast computer workload. They range from the intuitive subjective approach to the sophisticated mathematical models such as the Box-Jenkins method. In conducting workload forecasting, the forecaster must take into consideration the existence of factors that may cause abrupt change in the workload patterns. Technological advances such as the replacement of dumb terminals with intelligent terminals or personal computers capable of a certain amount of local computing may switch some workload from the mainframe CPU to the peripherals. It may also affect the traffic on the data communications network. Tuning of the system by moving workload from one component to another or from one time period to another may also cause changes in workload patterns. The forecaster must be aware of such changes in examining the historical data. Any planned or potential changes of this kind must also be accounted for in arriving at the final forecasts. In the following subsections, we describe a wide range of forecasting methods with an evaluation of their strengths and weaknesses.

2.6.2 Visual Trending

In the past, many computer installations used intuitive, informal, "seat-of-the-pants" approach in workload forecasting. They are based on the forecaster's personal perceptions of the specific circumstances he expects to be relevant during the forecast period (e.g., business expansion plan, budget increase, informal talk with user departments). The forecaster informally takes into account the influence of prevailing factors and implicitly weighs their relative importance according to his judgment. Subjective approach may produce excellent results if the firm is fortunate enough to have exceptionally gifted forecasters or the computer configuration is small and simple handling only a few applications. In general, however, there is a high risk of error in forecasting if a firm relies solely on gut feels and lucky guesses, especially when the computer system is complex and there are frequent changes in personnel (typical in data processing).

As the computer environment grows in complexity over a certain capacity level, it is no longer desirable nor perhaps even feasible to leave such a crucial exercise to just intuitive capabilities. Many installations therefore turn to historical workload data for help. The first step towards scientific forecasting is to organize these data either in the form of a plot or a table summarized into fixed time intervals. A visual inspection allows the forecaster to estimate the current growth rate and extrapolate it to the future projection. Other external factors such as business expansion plans and significant software and technological changes may still be incorporated into a final forecast. Anticipated new applications will also be added to arrive at a total projected workload for the forecast period. This method, although still largely subjective, does have some scientific basis, namely, the historical data and the current trend. It is an improvement over the haphazard, speculative type of purely subjective forecasting.

2.6.3 Time Series Regression Models

Time series forecasting models are based on the premise that the items to be forecasted (such as future workload) are somehow directly related to time or historical (workload) data. There are three main categories of time series models: regression models, moving averages models and Box-Jenkins models. We will outline regression models here and discuss moving averages and Box-Jenkins models later in separate subsections.

Regression models themselves include three main types: polynomial regression, sinusoidal regression, and autoregressive regression. The simplest form of a polynomial regression model is a straight line such as:

$$\hat{W}_t = a + bt, \qquad\qquad\qquad (2.5)$$

where $\hat{W}_t$ represents forecasted workload at time t, and 'a' and 'b' are constants estimated by the least squares method utilizing historical workload data.

Forecasting accuracy may sometimes be improved through the use of higher degree polynomials. Polynomial regression models should be used only for medium to long-range forecasts and should not normally go beyond the third degree [Chambers et al. 1971].

Polynomial regression models are appropriate where there is a long-term trend in the historical data. An inspection of a scatter diagram of the data usually indicates whether a particular polynomial model may describe the data. Although a higher degree polynomial model may improve the description, in practice a large part of the trend is usually explained by the linear and the quadratic terms.

The sinusoidal regression model is normally used to forecast seasonal or cyclical data. A typical sinusoidal model used to forecast monthly workload data is:

$$\hat{W}_t = a_1 + a_2 t + a_3 \, \text{sine}(2 \pi t/12) + a_4 \, \text{cosine}(2 \pi t/12), \qquad (2.6)$$

where $\hat{W}_t$ is forecasted workload, $\pi = 3.1416$, and the a's are the coefficients determined by the least squares method. The sine and cosine functions in the model are intended to capture the cyclical behaviors in the data, the second term t is intended to model a linear trend and a_1 is the mean of the time series.

Autoregressive regression models are appropriate when a stable relationship exists between adjacent observations in the time series. This type of model is applicable to the forecasting of computer resource demand due to the existing applications. The future demand of computer resources normally has a close relationship with the pattern of past demands. Therefore, we may use the following equation to anticipate the future demand in month t, i.e. $\hat{W}_t$:

$$\hat{W}_t = a_0 + a_1 \, W_{t-1} + a_2 \, W_{t-2} + \ldots + a_k \, W_{t-k}, \qquad (2.7)$$

where $W_{t-1}, \ldots, W_{t-k}$ are the actual demands for the item in the previous 'k' months and the a's are the coefficients determined by the least squares method.

2.6.4   Time Series Moving Averages Models

Two common forecasting methods, namely the simple moving averages model and the exponential smoothing model, are actually special cases of the autoregressive models.   That is, the coefficients a's are defined according to special constraints defined in these two models.   These coefficients may be estimated by constrained regression analysis or by some rules of thumb.

A moving average is simply a process of "updating." For example, a twelve-month period moving average assumes that the forecast for the next period is equal to the average of the previous twelve observations. (Of course, the forecaster should multiply this average by a coefficient to allow for growth.)   A major disadvantage of the simple moving average is that the same weight is given to the observations of the distant past as is given to the most recent observations.   However, the forecaster may modify the moving average model by allowing more recent observations to be weighed heavier in the calculation of the average. This modification yields what is commonly known as an exponentially weighted moving average (EWMA) model, or exponential smoothing.

Suppose a forecaster wishes to estimate workload in time t+1; the EWMA model will appear as:

$$\hat{W}_{t+1} = d\, W_t + d(1\text{-}d)\, W_{t-1} + d(1\text{-}d)^2\, W_{t-2} + d(1\text{-}d)^3\, W_{t-3} + \ldots$$
$$= \hat{W}_t + d(W_t - \hat{W}_t), \tag{2.8}$$

where d is called the smoothing constant ($0<d<1$), $\hat{W}_t$ and $\hat{W}_{t+1}$ are forecasted workload and W_t's are actual historical workload data.

Observe that decreasing weights are given to the older observations because the weights d, d(1-d), d(1-d)^2, etc., have decreasing magnitude. When d is close to one, the impact of older observed values is minimal.

Exponential smoothing models are good for short and medium-range forecasting in terms of cost-effectiveness [Groff 1973, and Makridakis et al. 1974]. A major disadvantage of exponential smoothing models is the uncertainty when choosing the appropriate value for d. This can be estimated through constrained regression analysis [Gill and Murray 1974]. Rules of thumb may also be used as Brown recommends [Brown 1963, p. 108]:

$$d = \frac{2}{(N + 1)} , \qquad (2.9)$$

where N is the number of periods in a cycle.

Mechanical calculations of the smoothing constant (d) must be modified by suitable guidelines. Some guidelines follow [Mendenhall and Reinmuth 1974, p.410]:

. If the underlying process is volatile, choose a small d, i.e., to assign weights more evenly over time.

. If the underlying process is stable, choose a large d, i.e., to weigh more heavily recent time points.

. The smoothing constant, d, should be such that the cost resulting from misforecasting is minimized.

In practice, a forecaster should experiment with several smoothing
constants and choose the best according to his test data. However, the
best current smoothing constant may not be suitable for the future.
Since the constant is intended to reflect the relative weight accorded
to the various past data, changes in their importance will necessitate a
review of the smoothing constant as well.   Therefore, a forecaster
should not be wedded forever to one smoothing constant.

2.6.5 Box-Jenkins Models

The Box-Jenkins (B-J) [Nelson 1973, Box and Jenkins 1976] method is
actually a philosophy for approaching forecasting situations. The method
postulates a generalized model which can describe the behavior of a
large variety of time series data. When the method is applied to a particular set of time series data, relevant parameters are selected from
the generalized model. This tentatively selected model is then tested
for its adequacy and if it proves acceptable, it will be used to develop
forecasts.   If not, the B-J process can indicate ways to improve the
tentative model for better forecasting. Thus, the B-J method provides a
rational, structured approach to the determination of an appropriate
forecasting model.

More specifically, the B-J method involves three basic steps. The
first is to select from a generalized model those parameters which are
necessary to describe the behavior of a given time series. The generalized model is as follows:

$$\hat{W}_t = a_1 W_{t-1} + a_2 W_{t-2} + \dots + a_p W_{t-p} - b_1 E_{t-1} - b_2 E_{t-2} - \dots - b_q E_{t-q},$$

$$(2.10)$$

where the W_t's are historical workload data, the E_t's are past forecast errors, and a's and b's are parameters to be estimated. From the pattern of the autocorrelations and partial autocorrelations of the time series, the B-J method would indicate which parameters should be included in the generalized model and how many lagged terms are necessary to describe the time series behavior. Since the pattern is not always obvious, however, professional judgment and experience are usually needed to select an appropriate model.

Once a tentative model has been selected, the second step would be to estimate the values of the parameters. Box and Jenkins proposed a non-linear least squares method which would estimate the parameters in such a way that forecast errors are minimized if the model selected is correct.

Finally, the B-J method provides explicit information to help the forecaster judge whether the tentative model adequately captures the behavior of the time series. This is done by checking the randomness of the forecast errors in the test data. If randomness is indicated, the tentative model is satisfactory and could be used to generate forecasts. If not, the pattern of the forecast errors would indicate possible improvements for the model and the forecaster would begin all over again from step one.

In summary, the B-J method provides the following desirable features:

(1)   It is versatile.   It may be used to forecast accurately time series data with divergent behavior.   In this respect, it is considered the most powerful forecating method available today.

(2)   It provides a systematic procedure which allows the forecaster to make incremental improvements in building his forecasting model and to arrive at a model that minimizes forecast errors.   The method further supplies information on the accuracy of future forecasts and provides signals if the existing model is becoming obsolete.

(3)   Once a model has been developed and accepted,   it is easy   to generate forecasts from it.

The major disadvantage of the B-J method is its complexity particularly in identifying a correct model.   Its usual requirement of 50 or more data points for reliable model identification can also be a problem for computer capacity planning since few companies have such long term data that is applicable for the current system environment. Because it is versatile and offers a complete system of forecasting, it is more complicated to use than individual techniques mentioned above. This difficulty is eased somewhat by the availability of statistical packages such as SAS [1985] and SPSS [1986].   However, these statistical packages often provide much better support on the univariate B-J model which is limited in scope for its application.   The B-J method also entails considerable costs in developing an appropriate model for a given set of data.   Even that, it may not provide the most accurate forecast under some circumstances [Chan and Ho 1986].

In the final analysis, it is up to the forecaster to decide whether the benefits of higher accuracy will compensate for the higher cost associated with the B-J method. For this reason, the B-J method should probably be used only when appropriate data is available and a high degree of forecasting accuracy is required.

2.6.6 Structural Models

Structural models are sets of mathematical formulae which purport to represent cause and effect relationships. Structural models need to be specified, that is, factors included in the models must be well defined. For example, the workload in time t (W_t) may be expressed in terms of user-oriented measures such as the number of users in time t (N_t) and budget in time t (B_t) in the following structural model:

$$\hat{W}_t = f(\ N_t,\ B_t\ ) \tag{2.11}$$

where f denotes a functional relationship between the predictors (N_t, B_t) and the forecasted variable ($\hat{W}_t$).

More and more installations have found use of structural models in forecasting computer workload, especially for large, stable production-type applications that have existed for quite some time and expected to remain in active use during the forecast period [Sarna 1979, Artis 1980, Bronner 1980]. Structural models may produce accurate forecasts when the cause and effect relationships are well known or can be established. The approach is especially appealing due to the general desire to express computer workload in terms of user-oriented measures which must be mapped to hardware-oriented measures for capacity planning.   Using this approach, forecasters must carefully examine the relevant factors that should be included in the model and also the relative influence of each of these factors.   Through this process of specification, it is likely that much pertinent information will be included when preparing the forecasts.

There are, however, at least two serious drawbacks associated with structural models so that care must be exercised in using them.   First, a structural model may not have been specified accurately.   Important factors may have been omitted or the functional relationships may not have been stated correctly.   For example, the model in (2.11) may have omitted the influence of latent workload.   Furthermore, the relevance and the importance of existing factors may be changing over time and thus the entire model could easily become outdated.

The second serious difficulty associated with structural models is that the future values of the predictors themselves must be forecasted. For example, to use the structural model shown in (2.11), the forecaster must first forecast the future values of N_t and B_t.   Obviously, an accurate prediction of W_t would be unlikely if the forecast of either predictor is inaccurate.

2.6.7 Technological Forecasting and the Delphi Method

Besides facility upgrade plans that can be implemented in the next couple of years, capacity planners are often required to lay out a longer term plan (say, five or more years) that provides a long term

direction for the installation to be matched against the enterprise-
level architecture developed through business systems planning or other
strategic planning methodologies [King 1978, Zachman 1986]. Long term
forecasting is often done through technological forecasting models.
Technological forecasting models use systems of logical analysis to
produce probabilistic forecasts of future technological developments.
Technological forecasting models normally include combinations of
subjective, structural, and time series models by the forecasters. We
include technological forecasting as a separate category to emphasize
the importance of these methods. They can be useful in times of revolu-
tionary technological change and shortage of resources such as what we
experience in the past 35 years of the entire computer age. The rapid
change in computer technology especially in the last few years is
evidenced by the increase in chip capacity, development in
telecommunications, decrease in hardware cost, and the widespread applications of computers in all walks of life [Pick 1986, pp.572-593].

The Delphi method is probably the best known of the technological
forecasting models [Fusfeld and Foster 1972, Linstone and Turoff, 1975].
The Delphi method involves a series of formal steps taken in an attempt
to obtain a consensus of "expert" opinions concerning some medium-range
or long-term events. Such a forecast will provide a capacity planner
with a long-term direction for his planning efforts. For example, knowing what services customers will likely demand from an industry (say,
banks) in five years, we can start mapping the kind of applications that
need to be developed and equipment that need to be added to the
configuration. The potential effect on workload growth due to these new

services can then be assessed.   The following Dephi procedure may be used to forecast service innovations:

(1) Letters are sent to a panel of "experts" (say 10 persons) asking them individually to name the service innovations they believe are both urgently needed and achievable in banking in the next five years. Each "expert" is asked to send his predictions back to the panel coordinator. A list of innovations (say 20 items) is compiled using these "expert" responses.

(2) The "experts" then each receive a list of the 20 items and are now requested to predict the timing when each innovation will occur within the next five-year period. The "experts" are again asked to send their estimates to the coordinator. Throughout this process, the "experts" work individually and are asked not to approach any other members of the panel. This arrangement allows independent estimates by the "experts."

(3) Letters are again sent to the "experts" informing them of the items upon which there is a general consensus and asking those who do not agree with the majority to state their reasons. For those items upon which there is no general consensus, each "expert" is requested to state the reasons for the divergent time estimates. As a result of these requests and responses, some "experts" can be expected to reevaluate their time estimates. This process of seeking consensus is repeated several times to narrow down the range of time estimates of occurrence for each innovation until a general consensus is reached. Thus, the company which uses this forecasting method could obtain con-

siderable information about service innovations in the coming years. Furthermore, because the method integrates human judgments in an objective manner, it often produces reliable results [Jensen 1979].

The results of the Delphi method and other technological forecasting models provide a long-term direction for the capacity planner so that the short- and medium-term plans can be steered towards that direction. These methods are by no means without disadvantages. The forecasting process may become ego trips for some of the "experts" who participate in the forecasting. In addition, a consensus may take a great deal of time to obtain. The specific role and the expertise required of the coordinator may be difficult to determine. Consequently, forecasters involved in technological forecasting must make certain that the procedures are properly planned and monitored and that the objectives of the forecast are not lost in the often long and complicated process of developing the forecasts.

2.6.8 User Survey

Contacting the users is an important way to forecast workload. With the reduction in sizes as well as prices, and the relaxation of environmental constraints, substantial amount of computer equipment can now be found in user department floors. These include computer terminals, printers, micro and even minicomputers. Many of them are purchased under the user department budget and under their control. Data centers are finding it more and more difficult to forecast the center's workload without knowing in advance the equipment to be installed in user areas. There are also other factors (e.g., budget) that may significantly influence computer usage. Consequently, there should be some attempts to obtain direct user input to the workload forecasting process.

In general, this approach involves the identification of major disjoint user groups, and the design of a questionnaire that solicits workload growth data in a language understandable by users. In order to help the user to make their own projections, historical workload data pertaining to each user group must be accurately prepared and clearly presented to the user along with the survey. Ideally, an average of the user's own projections weighted by each user group's usage may be used as the forecasted workload.

The major difficulty in this approach is two-fold. First, in the questionnaire, forecast must be requested in a user-oriented term (e.g., expected budget for internal computing, number of computer users, future plans in the use of existing applications as well as acquisition or development of new applications, etc.). The mapping of these projections into the quantities needed for the hardware-oriented workload forecast requires extensive modeling. Second, the identification of major user groups and the preparation of historical usage data by groups may not sound too difficult when a good resource accounting system is in place. However, the frequent changes in organizational structures make it difficult to relate historical usage data with the current organizational structures. In fact, forecasts by the newly formed organizational units may be pure guesses since there are few historical experiences to go by.

The main use of user survey should be the qualitative information provided by the users giving their plans concerning computing. This kind of information may be very useful for validating and/or adjusting the data center's own projections based on quantitative analysis of the historical as well as the new applications workload data.

2.7 Capacity Limits and Performance Objectives

2.7.1 Capacity Limits and Rules of Thumb

Capacity limit, here refers to the limit (or threshold) of utilizable capacity, is a point at which any additional workload is expected to result in excessive degradation of system performance. Traditionally, many rules of thumb have been relied on in determining the capacity limits of various components in a computer system. These rules of thumb attempt to relate overall system capacity to an individual component's capacity by defining what levels of utilization will prevent inordinate queueing delays of those resources which may impede the responsiveness of the system as a whole. For example, it is quite commonly accepted that the average CPU utilization of 80% and I/O channel utilization of 35% should not be exceeded so as to prevent excessive performance degradation.

A simple methodology based on the capacity limit rules of thumb is quite commonly used for computer performance evaluation and capacity upgrade decisions. Under this methodology, each key component on the

system is monitored and the utilization growth is tracked. Projected
utilization levels resulted from an extrapolation of the utilization
curve plus utilization estimated for new applications are compared to
the utilization threshold for each component. The point in time when
the projected utilization level exceeds the threshold is when system
changes are called for. Either a capacity upgrade of the component in
question or a system tuning may be required.

The advantages of this methodology are simplicity, ease of
understanding, and low cost. There are problems associated with the
method, however. The major ones are due to the exclusion of interaction
effects among different system components, the difficulty in giving dif-
ferential treatment to different types of workload, and the degree of
reliability with trend extrapolation. This methodology will be discussed in details in the component approach section of Chapter 3.

2.7.2 User-Oriented Performance Objectives

A computer installation may have a number of user-oriented performance objectives established. Some examples are:

. Interactive response time (e.g., for local user: average 2 seconds,
   95th percentile 5 seconds; for remote user: average 8 seconds, 95th
   percentile 20 seconds, etc.)

. Database inquiry response time (e.g., for local user: average 4
   seconds, 95th percentile 10 seconds; for remote user: average 10
   seconds, 95th percentile 30 seconds, etc.)

- Batch turnaround time (e.g., for short job class: average 20 minutes, 95th percentile 2 hours; for medium job class: average 1 hour, 95th percentile 8 hours; for long job class: average 4 hours, 95th percentile 24 hours, etc.)

- Printing turnaround time (e.g., for short output class: average 1 hour, 95th percentile 8 hours; for long output class: average 8 hours, 95th percentile 24 hours, etc.)

- System availability (e.g. 98% during each one-month period).

These performance objectives represent a standard of service levels the data center is committed to in offering the services to its users, and a yardstick that actual performance can be compared against. They are therefore also called service level objectives. They provide the user an indication of what to expect from the system. When actual performance does not meet these objectives, user complaints can be expected. Capacity saturation may have occurred in some components in the system, therefore action must be taken to correct the problem. Utilization measurements allow saturated components to be identified. Correction can then be made through workload balancing and/or capacity upgrade.

These performance objectives also represent key parameters in capacity planning, i.e., one can use these parameters to match against predicted future performance to identify performance problems before they occur and act to prevent them to happen. Performance can be related to utilization in a simple manner on a purely (or predominantly) interactive or batch system. Thus, CPU performance objective can be translated (with some approximations) into CPU utilization threshold which can then be used to arrive at the capacity limit in the planning process discussed in the above subsection. These performance objectives can be used directly as the decision parameters using a system modeling approach capacity planning methodology to be discussed in the next chapter.

One major issue in establishing performance objectives is what value should they be set to. Many installations will base on past performance experience in establishing their objectives. Some also rely on user feedback through discussions and negotiations with major user groups. User productivity as well as computer costs are two major considerations in setting up these service-level objectives.

The effect of terminal response time on user productivity has been of great interest among researchers and practitioners. It is known that the effect is different for different types of work performed on the terminal. The actual impact can be assessed through an extensive productivity study of the organization's various groups of terminal users. Corporate management ought to weigh carefully the costs and benefits of performing such a productivity study to derive an appropriate response time objective.

Performance objectives are not to be set once and for all. They should be reviewed regularly. One major factor for their revisions is a change in user requirements. This often happens when a competitor company has or is expected to offer improved services to its customers through the use of advanced equipment. To maintain the competition, users may demand equivalent performance from the computer as in the competitor company. Performance objectives should therefore be modified accordingly.

2.8 Performance Prediction

A main goal of computer capacity planning is to be able to determine the amounts of capacity that will be needed in the future to process the expected workloads with the required levels of service. Implicit in this goal is that we must forecast workload and predict system performance. Various schemes for workload forecasting have been presented earlier. Several methods for predicting performance will be outlined below. Methods available range from the simple trending approach to the complex queueing network modeling to the classical simulation modeling.

2.8.1 Trending

This is perhaps the most intuitive and simple approach in performance prediction. Performance and workload are monitored and recorded historically. With sufficient amount of measured data we can plot a graph of performance versus workload from which hopefully a clear trend can be identified. An extrapolation of the trend to the projected workload level is used as the predicted performance.

This method is intuitive, easy to understand, fast to implement, and requires little special tools or facilities. In many cases, it does produce credible results, especially when the system is largely under-utilized. There are several problems with this approach, however. First, the method assumes that the trend at the higher end of workload follows that at the current lower workload level. This assumption may be far from being true, especially when the projected workload level is much higher than current. When workload increases to a certain level, some system components will become bottlenecks and performance will degrade drastically. Therefore, performance predicted based on the current trend tends to be overly optimistic. Second, the graph of performance versus workload may not exhibit a clear trend historically. It will often be a scatter diagram from which a possible trend is to be estimated. Regression techniques may be used to attempt the trend identification. Any error made in this identification will be magnified in the extrapolated region thus producing unreliable predictions. Third, most installations have a number of different workload types each of which must be measured separately for workload and performance. Examples include interactive, batch of different classes (e.g., short, medium, and long job classes), database inquiry and update, etc. For each type of workload, a separate graph has to be produced and its performance predicted. Using this trending approach, prediction of performance for each workload type is done as if it is the only workload in the system. Interaction effect has been ignored, when in fact the performance of one workload type can degrade simply due to workload increase in another workload type. The result again is an underestimation of performance degradation.

2.8.2   Queueing Models

A branch of applied probability theory known as "queueing theory"
has been used extensively in the literature for the analysis and prediction of computer system performance. (See for example, Gordon and
Newell [1967], Kleinrock [1976], Courtois [1977], Allen [1978], and
Sauer and Chandy [1981]). Queueing models in performance analysis are
sets of mathematical formulae which are devised to capture the relationships between workload and performance measures. Taking into consideration of the probabilistic nature of the arrival times and the size of
the incoming work, expected values and distributions of performance
measures can be derived. This method of analysis is often referred to
as analytic modeling.

A basic queueing model of a computer system consists of a source of
potential customers (the incoming work such as a job, an inquiry, etc.),
one or more waiting lines (the queues), and one or more service centers
(also called servers, e.g., a CPU, an I/O channel). In more complex
models, the output from one server may become input to other servers
forming a network of queues. Queueing network models will be discussed
in the next subsection.

A queueing system may be described by the Kendall [1953] notation
which has the form A/B/C, where A specifies the interarrival time
distribution, B specifies the service time distribution, and C specifies
the number of servers. For example, a M/M/1 system has an exponential
interarrival time distribution (more commonly known as Poisson arrival),
exponential service time distribution, and a single service center.

Other symbols that may be used for A and B in the notation include: D for Deterministic distribution, G for General Independent distribution, and Ek for Erlangian-k distribution.

The specification of the interarrival time and service time distributions define the workload. For example, with a mean of n arrivals per second and a mean service time E(s) seconds, utilization, the fraction of time the server is expected to be busy is:

$$u = n\ E(s),\qquad\qquad\qquad (2.12)$$

Suppose we are interested in the response time for jobs executed in this system. The expected response time R on a M/M/1 and a M/G/1 systems can be obtained from (2.13) and (2.14), respectively.

$$R = \frac{E(s)}{1 - u}\qquad\qquad\qquad (2.13)$$

$$R = E(s) + \frac{uE(s)}{2(1 - u)}\ [1 + (\frac{V(s)}{E(s)^2})\ ]\qquad (2.14)$$

where V(s) is the variance of the service time.

These formulae apply to any job dispatching discipline provided that its selection of the next job to be serviced does not depend on the service time and that each job is serviced to completion before the next job is dispatched. For servers such as CPU where jobs time-share the CPU using a round-robin scheduling discipline, the response time on both M/M/1 and M/G/1 systems is given by (2.13). (The derivation of this formula assumes that the time quantum received by a job in each cycle through the server is infinitely small. Such a scheduling discipline is commonly called processor sharing [Kleinrock 1976, pp. 166-170].)

When workload is composed of several workload classes, priority scheduling is often used to give preferred treatment to certain classes (e.g., interactive class has higher priority over batch job classes). In such a system, the response time of jobs at lower priority levels is a function of the loading, service, and utilization of the given level and all higher priority levels. The response times at the various priority levels are given as follows:

$$R_1 = \frac{1}{1} \left[E(s_1) + \frac{E(s_1)u_1}{1 - u_1} \right]$$

$$R_2 = \frac{1}{1 - u_1} \left[E(s_2) + \frac{E(s_1)u_1 + E(s_2)u_2}{1 - (u_1 + u_2)} \right] \quad (2.15)$$

$$R_3 = \frac{1}{1 - (u_1 + u_2)} \left[E(s_3) + \frac{E(s_1)u_1 + E(s_2)u_2 + E(s_3)u_3}{1 - (u_1 + u_2 + u_3)} \right]$$

and so forth, where R_i is the response time, $E(s_i)$ is the mean service time and u_i is the server utilization factor attributed to the workload at priority level i (level 1 being the highest priority).

Many results are available giving performance prediction of the single server queueing model using different scheduling discipline under various constraints. A comprehensive survey can be found in Kleinrock [1976].

In a computer system, a job requires the service from several resources (CPU, channel, I/O device, etc.) for its completion. The time spent at each resource must be accumulated to determine the total time the job is in the system. The representation of a job's progress in a computer system as stages of queues without feedback has certain theoretical inaccuracies. The simplicity of the approach and the robustness of the formulae have made it a viable approach, however.

2.8.3 Queueing Network Models

As pointed out above, a more appropriate model for computer systems is one which accounts for multiple resources (service centers). A job exiting from one service center can become input to the queues of other service centers in the system, forming a network of queues. A typical queueing network model with a terminal-driven workload is given in Figure 2.1. Each circle represents a service center and the rectangles represent the queues. Specification of the model may include parameters such as average user think time, average service times on the CPU, on Disk 1, and on Disk 2, etc.

With specific parameter values, it is possible to evaluate performance measures of interest by solving some simple equations. For example, suppose we are given that average terminal user think time Z is 15 seconds, terminal throughput X is 0.87 transactions/second, and that M=20 users are logged in. Then the terminal response time can be obtained by the interactive response time formula

$$R = M/X - Z \qquad\qquad (2.16)$$

$$= 8 \text{ seconds}$$

Suppose our forecast indicates that the number of users logged in will

Figure 2.1

A QUEUEING NETWORK MODEL
WITH A TERMINAL-DRIVEN WORKLOAD

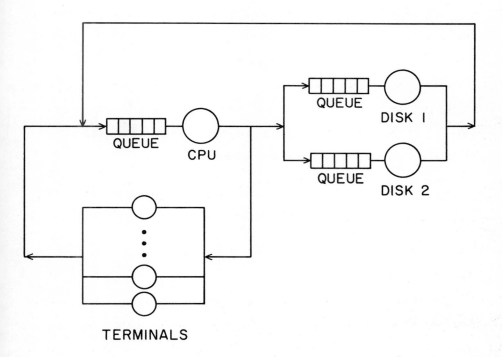

TERMINALS

increase to 25.   To find out if the 8-second response time is still feasible, we use the response time asymtote formula

$$R \geq M \, D_b - Z \qquad\qquad (2.17)$$

where b refers to any device that is capable of saturating (bottleneck device) as workload increases, and D_b is the service demand (average time required to service a transaction) on the bottleneck device.   In this example, suppose the bottleneck device is the CPU, and that D_{CPU} is 1 second, then solving equation (2.17) gives R $\geq$10 seconds. This implies that an 8-second response is no longer feasible under the new load.   To yield the desired response time we need a faster CPU that gives service time D'_{CPU}. That is, we need

or

$$M \, D'_{CPU} - Z \leq 8 \text{ seconds}$$

$$D'_{CPU} \leq 0.92 \text{ seconds.} \qquad\qquad (2.18)$$

The CPU required is therefore $1/0.92 = 1.09$, that is, 9% faster than the current CPU.

The above example is based on the operational analysis treatment of queueing network modeling which was developed by Buzen and Denning [Buzen 1976, Buzen and Denning 1978].   This is an alternative approach to the stochastic analysis of queueing network modeling that was studied by Jackson [1954] and many others [See for example, Coffman and Kleinrock 1968, Coffman et al. 1970, Baskett et al. 1975, Kleinrock 1976]. The stochastic approach is based on concepts such as steady state, ergodicity, independence and the distribution of specific random variables.   The operational analysis approach, on the other hand, is based on directly measurable quantities and other assumptions such as flow balance and homogeneity. In many aspects of computer performance analysis, neither approach offers advantages over the other. The operational analysis does have one benefit, that is, quantities involved are directly measurable and the results need not be derived using advanced queueing theory, thus making them more easily understandable and applied. (For a more detailed discussion on these two approaches, see Denning and Buzen [1978] and Muntz [1978].)

Queueing network modeling can be viewed as a subset of the techniques in queueing theory. Much of queueing theory is oriented towards modeling a complex system using a single service center with complex characteristics. Relatively detailed performance measures can be obtained from these models (e.g., distribution as well as averages). Queueing network modeling, on the other hand, uses networks of service centers with simple characteristics in the models. Depending on the focus of the particular analysis on hand, an appropriate set of service centers can be selected, the relationships between the input and output of these service centers defined, and the performance measures can then be evaluated. Many algorithms developed in queueing network modeling relate readily with quantities measurable from hardware and/or software monitors. Software packages can therefore be developed to allow the use of queueing network models in performance analysis and to perform predictions requiring only a basic understanding of the underlying theory. Some commercially available performance medeling packages are: BEST/1 by BGS Systems [1982], MAP by Quantitative System Performance [1982], and PAWS/A by Information Research Associates [1983].

2.8.4 Simulation Models

A simulation model is a program or set of programs (simulator)
written to represent the dynamic behavior of a system by reproducing its
states and corresponding state transitions. Simulation models have the
capability to model computer systems at any desired level of details and
are therefore powerful tools in system analysis.

Like analytic modeling, simulation is a prediction tool. For performance prediction, there are two aspects of the system that can be
simulated: the future workload and the future system configuration. The
simulation of the future workload is sometimes referred to as a synthetic workload. Execution of a synthetic workload (synthetic load
benchmarking) on the existing system allows us to answer questions such
as, "How much growth in workload is possible before the current capacity
is exceeded?" The creation of a synthetic workload typically involves:

(1) Trace terminal activities, recording a script of the jobs (may
be commands, transactions, or batch programs) submitted to the system.

(2) A program is written to simulate the generation of commands and
program submissions based on the script obtained in (1). Such a simulation program is usually called a driver. Parameters can be built-in to
allow for the simulation of increased workload.

(3) The simulation of terminal activity is transparent to the application programs. Therefore, the application programs are executed as
normal, as driven by the driver. Performance measures can then be
measured, at any desired workload levels. Since application programs
are actually executed at the rate that represents the future workload,

performance can be accurately measured. If the increased load as generated by the driver correctly models the future workload, this approach will provide accurate performance prediction. It should be noted that if stress conditions are to be tested (i.e., the point at which the system's throughput slows down due to saturation in some system components), the driver must reside on a separate processor that is fast enough so that it will not saturate before the processor under test.

The need for simulating future system configurations for performance prediction arises when the system to be studied does not yet exist. For example, suppose we have determined that the current system configuration will become saturated in the near future and the CPU and the data communications network are expected to be the bottlenecks. We may then wish to investigate the relative merits of several proposals which consist of upgrading the CPU to different models and the communication network in different ways. A simulator may be constructed that allows the CPU capacity and the network configuration to be specified as the model parameters. Simulated workload will be input to the simulator. Output of the simulator should include all performance measures of interest. The choice of what measures to output and at what level of details is that of the simulation model designer. The more data required and details produced, the more costly it is to construct and to run a simulation model. But the more detailed and accurate prediction obtained from the model may allow a more cost-effective capacity plan to be drawn up, thus achieving considerable cost savings. The capacity planner therefore must make trade-offs by keeping an ap-

propriate balance between accuracy and efficiency. More detailed discussions on simulation modeling can be found in Gordon [1978].

The major weakness of simulation modeling is its relative cost. It
usually involves the writing and debugging of a complex computer
program, collecting and validating data on a large number of parameters,
and the running of a lengthy program that requires substantial computational resources. The availabilty of computer simulation program
packages (e.g., SAM, CASE) that generate the simulation program from a
model description helps simplify the task. A technique known as hybrid
modeling takes advantage of both analytic and simulation modeling. It
employs analytic modeling wherever possible and resorts to simulation
only for the parts where analytic results are not available or do not
provide detailed measures as required.

2.9 Summary

Computer capacity planning should be an ongoing and reiterative
process with the long-term objective of providing computer services to
the installation's users in a cost-effective manner. There should be a
systematic methodology that enables the computer center's management to
make timely and informed decisions regarding the upgrade and change of
computer facilities.

A number of tasks are involved which include: maintain an up-to-
date inventory of the installation's hardware and software facilities,
define workload measures and identify the installation's workload

characteristics, define performance indexes of interest to the installation from both user and computer center management perspectives, decide on the scheme to be used for workload and performance data collection (continuous, sampled, or ad hoc) and data analysis (all or sampled), select hardware and software monitoring tools for workload and performance measurements, perform workload forecasting, determine capacity limits of current configuration and performance objectives, and undertake performance predictions. This chapter has outlined for each of these tasks: what needs to be done, major problems one may expect to encounter, common approaches for implementing each task, and an assessment of these approaches. In the next chapter, these tasks will be integrated to illustrate how a systematic capacity planning process can be carried out using currently available techniques and tools.

CHAPTER 3

COMPONENT VERSUS SYSTEM MODELING APPROACH

3.1 Introduction

A successful capacity plan relies on a good understanding of the installation's current system environment and a reliable projection of the installation's future computing needs. The many tasks involved in the process and the various techniques for carrying them out have been discussed in Chapter 2. How extensive the entire process is and how involved each task is depend on the approach taken by the installation.

Often times some ask, "With the rapid decline in cost and increase in capability, why don't we solve the capacity shortage problem by simply adding more equipment which are probably less expensive than spending high-salaried personnel time in detailed system analysis for an upgrade solution?" The fallacy of this approach is two-fold. First, even though the cost per instruction execution is falling rapidly, the amount of money spent on computing is rising (mainly due to increased computerization). Computing budget growth of 20% per annum is not uncommon. Computing budget comes from the same pool of funds as all

69

other budgets (e.g., production, marketing, etc.), therefore must compete for its allocation. Budget increase requires good justification which is only possible with a good understanding of the system (present and future). Second, knowledge of the system not only enables a cost-effective capacity upgrade plan to be drawn up, but also allows system tuning that results in more efficient execution of the same workload. Simple system tuning efforts such as balance of workload, change of blocking factors, relocation of files, restructuring of application programs, and so on, often lead to better utilization of the existing system, thus delaying an otherwise obvious need for upgrade. When judiciously undertaken, substantial cost savings are often achieved through such efforts.

In this chapter we shall present two different approaches for the implementation of the capacity planning process, a component approach and a system modeling approach. The component approach is fast and simple to implement. With simple measurement data, trend extrapolations and rules of thumb, capacity planners can often come up with reasonable plans. The system modeling approach is based on modeling which is an attempt to extract the essential aspects of the system's operational characteristics and represent them in mathematical formulae, computer programs, or both. The system modeling approach is flexible in that it can be implemented at any desired level of details. It is methodical in that it enforces the gathering, organizing, evaluation, and understanding of information about a computer system. Once constructed, the model can provide great insight about the system and can be used to predict system behavior under future scenarios. It can therefore be a very useful capacity planning tool. The component and system modeling approaches will be discussed in detail below.

3.2 A component Approach

This approach consists of the same basic tasks as described in Chapter 2. In the implementation of each task, however, the more intuitive alternative is used.

The underlying concept of this approach is that each component in a computer system is treated largely as an independent unit, including the CPU, memory, I/O channels, disks, printers, etc. The capacity of the CPU, for example, is usually defined as the utilizable CPU hours available per day, per week, per month, etc., taking into account the hours of operation, scheduled maintenance, unscheduled system down time due to hardware or software failures, reruns due to human or machine errors, capacity limit rules of thumb, and so forth.

Due to differences in speed and other features (cache memory size, virtual to physical address mapping, etc.), a CPU hour in one CPU model is not equivalent to an hour in another CPU model. Capacity limit on a faster CPU model must therefore be adjusted by a factor that reflects its power relative to the slower CPU. One measure for the comparison of CPU power is MIPS (Millions of Instructions Per Second). The comparison is based on the concept of instruction mix which gives the relative instruction execution frequencies that correspond to those in a typical workload. The MIPS rating of a CPU gives the number of millions of in-

structions the machine is capable of executing in a second given an instruction mix. For example, an approximate MIPS rating of 2.67 for IBM
3033S means that the machine is expected to execute 2.67 millions of instructions per second in a typical workload. Knowing also that an IBM
4341 has a MIPS rating of 0.82, we may say that an IBM 3033S is
2.67/0.82, or approximately 3.3 times faster than an IBM 4341 assuming
identical instruction mixes. Using this factor, we can then define the
capacity limit of an IBM 3033S as approximately 3.3 times that of an IBM
4341. Benchmarking can also be used to compare power of different CPUs.

A capacity plan outlining what and when upgrades of the existing
system need to be made, begins with a capacity study to identify such
needs. Capacity studies are to be conducted regularly as part of the
on-going planning process. They may also be initiated due to lease expiration of some components, major software changes, planned implementation of new applications, change in user requirements, and anticipated
technological advances. In the following we will present a typical procedure for a capacity study using the component approach, apply this
procedure in an example, and discuss the merits and pitfalls of the
approach.

3.2.1 A Capacity Study Procedure - Component Approach

In its simplest form, a capacity study using this approach may proceed as follows:

(1) Track the CPU hours consumed using data collected by the accounting monitor on the system.

(2) Plot the monthly (or weekly, daily, etc.) CPU-hour consumption over time as shown in Figure 3.1. The graph in Figure 3.1 also shows the capacity limit on the current system which is calculated based on some rules of thumb either established through past experience or from industry-wide experience. It is obvious that 100% utilization is impossible. Our experience indicates that a utilization threshold within the 60-80% range is typical after considering such factors as system down time, operational problems, error recovery, workload characteristics, service level requirements, etc. Multiplying the total hours of operations by the threshold percentage gives the utilizable CPU capacity limit for the CPU in consideration.

(3) Workload is forecasted based on an extrapolation of a trend visually or scientifically identified from the graph. New applications, new software environment, and new user requirements are also considered in arriving at the workload projection. The projected workload is shown in Figure 3.1 as the dotted curve. The point at which the current capacity limit and the projected workload curve intersect is where the current capacity is expected to be exceeded. An upgrade should therefore be planned for that time (i.e., July 1987 in the example).

(4) Other components on the system such as I/O channels, peripheral devices, front end communications controllers, and so on, are also monitored for their utilization. The utilization data are also tracked and projected. For disk systems the usage is often in terms of storage space occupied (e.g., MB or million bytes). Rules of thumb giving utilization thresholds for these components are observed for the determination of upgrade points.

Figure 3.1

SAMPLE WORKLOAD GRAPH

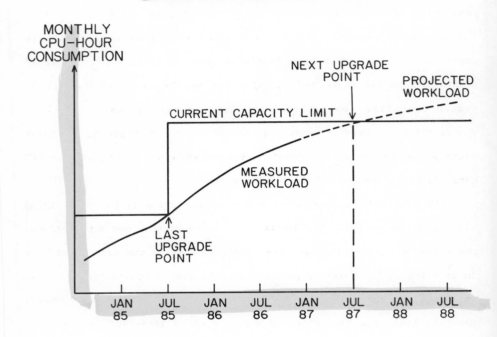

3.2.2   Refinements to the Procedure

Refinements may be made to the above basic procedure to account for the differences in the characteristics of the workload, the availability of measurement data due to the use of certain monitors, the desired level of details for the results from the capacity study, and so on.   Some of the more important refinements are explained below.

Use of Day Time or Peak Time Workload

Many installations are finding themselves with rapidly increasing demand for online services such as time-sharing, transaction processing, database inquiry, etc.   By their very nature, these services are needed during the day time office working hours (e.g., 8 a.m. to 5 p.m.) and must be satisfied as soon as possible (i.e., cannot wait overnight).   In yet other organizations, there are several hours in each day when peak demands for computer services are experienced.   During these hours computer performance has the most exposure.   Under these circumstances, planning should be done mainly based on the day time or peak time workload.   Most software monitors and resource accounting monitors allow the identification of the arrival and completion times of each job or transaction.   Workload and capacity limit during these selected hours of operation can be calculated and plotted similar to Figure 3.1.   This may be used as a replacement or a supplement to the full day capacity analysis discussed above.

Technological Upgrade

If the capacity study is initiated by a known or anticipated technological advance in (or lease expiration of) the CPU or other key
components, then the study should continue with a cost and benefits
analysis even if the workload is not expected to exceed the current
capacity within the forecast period. The cost and benefits analysis is
required to assess the viability of replacing the current equipment with
the more advanced product. If the analysis shows that such a replacement is cost justified considering all the costs involved and the
benefits to be gained, then an upgrade can be recommended.

Upgrade Versus Tuning

The conclusion of the above procedure arriving at the timing of
upgrade for the system components is based on an assumption that the
system is well tuned.   That is, system parameters (multiprogramming
level, scheduling policy, etc.) are set properly, files are allocated
optimally, workload for different equipment units of the same type is
well balanced, program execution is spread throughout the day, the week,
the month, and the year, as much as possible, and operations personnel
scheduled optimally. It is true that most installations are far from
these ideal conditions. However, it is also true that most installations have on-going tuning processes that deal with short-term and local
changes that can result in improvement in the operation of the system.
It is therefore reasonable to assume that the system is or will be tuned
as much as it can be (with consideration of human factors as well). Any
improvements over the current setting through tuning may allow the cur-

rent configuration to stretch beyond the projected upgrade point. A safety valve can therefore be added to the basic procedure by requiring that any capacity study that concludes with an upgrade plan should always initiate a detailed examination of the efficiency of the existing system. Any room for further tuning should be formulated as an alternative to be included in the cost and benefits analysis of the proposal for system changes.

Adjustment of Workload Data Due to Tuning

One common action taken in computer system tuning is to move workload around. The move can be from one equipment unit to another. For example, files moved from one disk drive to another can help balance the space occupancy and/or access frequencies on various drives. The move can also be from one time peiod to another. For example, some batch programs submitted during the day can be given a "hold" class so that they will not be executed until a pre-scheduled time (e.g., after 5 p.m.). This workload balancing has a great impact on the tracking of workload, especially when the workload to be considered is only for certain selected hours (e.g., peak hours) of a day. The CPU-hour consumption as recorded and summarized for the peak hours may show a significant drop from one month to another, not due to a decrease of workload but due to a tuning effort. Therefore, injudicious use of these data will likely lead to incorrect conclusions.

If the programs or files that have been moved can be identified in the monitored data, then the previously measured workload data can be adjusted by removing these programs or files from the previous

statistics. However, such an identification may not always be possible.
For example, the monitor used for workload and performance measurement
may not distinguish the jobs, or the new batch job class (e.g., the
"hold" class) may have never existed before. In this case, the amount
of workload moved must be estimated and the historical workload measurement data adjusted accordingly. The revised workload measurement should
provide more reasonable data for trending.

Breakdown by Workload Component

Most installations have several components of workload, typically
including a component for interactive service, one for transaction and
database processing, and one or more for different classes of batch
jobs. Data collected by most accounting monitors or software monitors
allow the breakdown of workload by component. Therefore CPU-hour consumption by component can be monitored separately and a trend can be
identified and extrapolated individually. The advantage of doing this
is that the difference in the growth of different workload classes can
be accounted for. As before, the total CPU consumption by all workload
components (present and projected) is plotted and compared against the
CPU capacity limit.

Projection of New Applications

The forecasted workload from trend extrapolation normally reflects
the growth due to existing applications only. For installations that
have large application projects under development or anticipate the purchase of new software packages, and expect to have them implemented

within the forecast horizon, the workload due to the new applications must be projected separately. An intuitive method to project this is based on existing applications. For instance, suppose the new application is to be implemented in the existing transaction processing subsystem (e.g., a CICS application on an IBM system). This application is expected to add 20 users to the system initially and 5 more users per year for the next 3 years. The existing transaction processing subsystem has 200 active users and is consuming 30 CPU hours per month with the fixed overhead portion removed. The CPU-hour consumption per transaction processing user is then estimated as 30/200, or 0.15 hours. The new application is then estimated with an initial workload of 0.15x20, or 3 CPU hours per month.

High-Medium-Low Projections

To allow for the estimation of uncertainties in workload forecasts, some installations may make high, medium and low projections. The high projection represents an optimistic forecast, obtained by extrapolating from a faster growing portion of the workload graph, a more optimistic estimate of the development project completion date, a higher expectation of the budget approval, and so forth. The low projection represents a pessimistic forecast, obtained by taking the opposite view as above. The medium projection represents the most likely forecast and is the one to be used in carrying out the complete analysis and arriving at a capacity plan proposal. The high and low projections can be used for sensitivity analysis to determine how flexible the plan is when things do not turn out as expected. If the cost and benefits conclusion is reversed under these alternative projections, then the proposed plan may not be as beneficial as it might appear and should be accordingly modified when feasible.

3.2.3 An Example

The system being considered has a single CPU with a disk subsystem supporting the organization's online transaction processing and application development activities, and other standard peripherals such as tape drives, printers, and terminals. The system's workload is therefore composed of three components: an online service for data entry and inquiry, an interactive and a batch service mainly for software development.

Using the above procedure, the CPU-hour consumption recorded by the hardware, software, or accounting monitor will be used as the basis of workload measure on the CPU. If accounting monitor is used, with the operating system overhead properly distributed, the CPU-hour consumption by each workload component can be obtained.

Since the system's main objective is to support the online service required for the business operation, the installation wants to provide adequate service during peak load business hours which consist of two hours in the morning and two in the afternoon. Therefore the computer workload during these four hours in 20 working days of each month is measured. This monthly peak hour CPU consumption is plotted over time as shown in Figure 3.2. The workload curve in the figure consists of two portions: the solid portion represents the measured CPU-hour consum-

Figure 3.2

WORKLOAD VERSUS CAPACITY

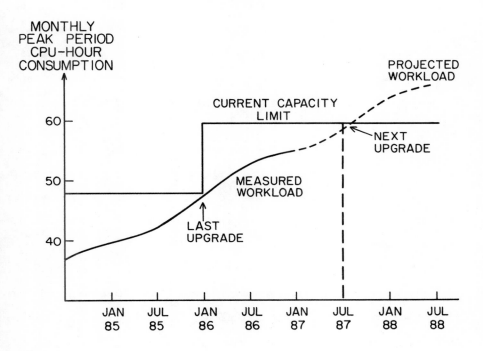

ption and the dotted portion represents the projected requirement. The projection is based on an extrapolation of the current trend. The figure also shows the capacity limit of the current configuration, based on a rule of thumb of a 75% utilization threshold. That is, it is assumed that system performance in terms of response time will degrade to an unsatisfactory level when the average CPU utilization exceeds 75%. With the peak hour operation of 4 hours a day, 20 days a month, and a 75% utilization threshold, the capacity limit is 4x20x75% = 60 hours per month.

The comparison between the projected workload and capacity limit indicates that the workload level will exceed the capacity limit in about July 1987. Upgrade of the CPU should therefore be planned for that time, or compensation steps should be taken to reduce workload during the peak-period operation.

All other components in the system are also monitored for their utilizations during the peak operation hours. When the average utilization of a component is projected to exceed its predetermined utilization threshold, then an upgrade plan can be in order.

Due to on-going tuning effort in the installation, workload has been moved from day time to night shift, and from one component to another (i.e., some files have been moved from one disk drive to another, or archived to tapes). As a result, utilization levels monitored for the peak hours do not provide accurate trends. Furthermore, the monitor used to measure utilization of the peripheral components does not allow the association of utilization to the jobs that incur it. Therefore no adjustment to the previously measured utilization can be made to permit meaningful trending. An accurate trend on the growth of utilization levels on a component enables a projection of future utilization levels on the component. Lack of a useful trend to rely on, an alternative projection of these components' future utilization levels can be made based on the growth rate of CPU-hour consumption.

Again, the conclusion of an upgrade plan based on the result of a capacity study assumes that the system is well tuned. If there is room for tuning then the upgrade can often be postponed. Therefore the in-itiation of a major upgrade plan should trigger a tuning study to deter-mine if efficiency can be sufficiently improved to warrant further pursuit. The result of such a tuning study will be included as an al-ternative to be analyzed in the proposal for system changes.

3.2.4 Strengths and Weaknesses

This component approach has the advantage of being simple and easy to understand. It follows our intuition that when a resource is "fully" utilized then additional resources will be needed. The implementation of computer capacity planning using this approach does not require very special tools aside from a resource accounting monitor, and possibly some simple software monitors; nor does it require a large number of staff. It is therefore relatively inexpensive to provide a capacity planning function based on a procedure as given above. As a result, it may be a suitable approach for smaller installations, as well as for starting a formal capacity planning function in a more complex computer installation.

This approach, however, has some major weaknesses including:

(1)   Since each component is monitored independently of each other, the effect of saturation in one component on another will not be reflected in these measurements, and will be difficult to fully understand. To ensure that system performance will be largely satisfactory to users, capacity limits on individual components tend to be set sufficiently low so that system performance will not degrade drastically due to this lack of understanding. The consequence may then be over capacity.

(2)   This approach is based on a theory that when utilization of a resource reaches a certain threshold, the queue builds up rapidly. Consequently response time or turnaround time for service on this resource may become unacceptably long for all types of workload including time-sharing, database inquiry, batch processing, etc. However, the effect of queueing on different types of workload may be very different. For example, response time for the time-sharing service will become unacceptable at much lower levels of utilization than batch. With the component approach, however, only one utilization threshold can be used for a given component in the upgrade decision. The utilization threshold that is proper for the interactive workload is likely to be too low for batch processing. A conservative setting of the utilization threshold will make it too low for most workload type. The result again may be over capacity.

(3)   Different components exhibit very different performance be-

havior when workload increases.   For instance, I/O channels exhibit
queueing at very low level of utilization (e.g., 35%) while the CPU is
able to perform satisfactorily under much higher level of utilization
(e.g., 75%).   This is why different utilization thresholds should be
used for different components.   Rules of thumb for utilization threshold
on different component are in fact often used.   These rules of thumb may
not be applicable to every installation, however.   The determination of
installation dependent rules of thumb   requires extensive analysis of
historical data to correlate each component's utilization levels with
performance measures including terminal response time and batch turnaround time.   For installations that rely on industry-wide rules of
thumb, specific performance requirements on individual installations due
to their unique workload mix cannot be incorporated in the upgrade decision rules using this approach.

(4)   The projection on the levels of utilization under future
workload are done mainly through trend extrapolation in this approach.
The problem with trend extrapolation is two-fold.   First, the trend may
not be easily identifiable.   The historical data sometimes result in a
scatter diagram with no clear-cut trend patterns.   Any error in the
identification of the current trend will be magnified in the extrapolation region.   Second, the use of trend extrapolation for projection is
based on the assumption that the future follows the current trend.   How
valid is this assumption depends on the length of the historical data
used, and the degree of resemblance between the future and current
(historical) environment.   If the conditions under which the system
operates change drastically (economy slows down, business reduces,

budget cuts back, etc.), then the current trend is most likely not a good predictor. Erroneous projections will result in incorrect upgrade decisions.

3.2.5 Beyond the Capacity Study

Once the need and timing for upgrade are established, then alternatives will be examined. The alternatives will include the various upgrade options. They should also include tuning options, if any have been identified. Most organizations will also include a "do-nothing" option to be considered among other alternatives.

A proposal must outline all options, and for each option list all additional resources required (include hardware, software, personnel, services, etc.), provide details for all estimated costs and expected benefits, and a justification for the selected option. After the proposal is approved by appropriate levels of management, the selection and acquisition process begins. The process generally includes the following steps:

(1)   Send requests for proposals to potential suppliers, giving specifications of mandatory requirements and desirable requirements.

(2)   Examine all the proposals that are received prior to the deadline, and discard the ones that do not satisfy all the mandatory requirements.

(3)   Evaluate the remaining proposals financially. All the costs involved in implementing each proposal must be identified over a study period. (The length of a study period is determined by considering the

expected life cycle of the component in question.) The costs include all one-time costs (purchase, installation, conversion, training, software, etc.) and on-going costs (maintenance, operations, supplies, etc.). Different financing options such as purchase versus lease versus rental must also be compared. Benefits to be considered in the analysis should include tangible (e.g., reduction of personnel, reduction of telephone cost) and intangible benefits (e.g., faster response time for programmers, improved service to customers).

These steps are required whether the upgrade decision is arrived at using the component approach, or a system modeling approach which will be discussed in the next section.

3.3 A System Modeling Approach

3.3.1 Why System Modeling

The major weaknesses of the component approach discussed above are due to the inconsistency between the objective of a computer installation and the way it is evaluated. The overall mission of a computer installation is to provide service to the user community. How well is the existing facility fulfilling this mission should be judged based on performance indexes defined from the user perspective (e.g., terminal response time, batch turnaround time). The same index should also be employed in decisions related to when and what changes need to be done to the existing facility so that satisfactory services to the users can be maintained.

Response time and turnaround time as experienced by the users are the results of a group of interconnected resources working together as a system in servicing user requests. They can be measured readily on the existing system configuration using hardware, software, or resource accounting monitors. For the purpose of capacity planning these measure must be projected into the future with respect to the forecasted workload. The component approach, however, does not lend itself to producing such projections in any direct and convincing way. As a result, many installations find their capacity planning process to be reactionary at times since they do not predict the performance degradation early enough. And at other times, they may find their systems to be over-configured simply by keeping their system components to be within the predetermined utilization thresholds.

To be able to predict system performance in the future, we need to identify, from the extremely complex hardware and software structures, those behaviors that are most sensitive to workload changes. The representation of these system behaviors in a form that can be solved mathematically will result in an analytic model. A representation in a form that "mimics" the real process, often by means of computer programs, will result in a simulation model, and a combination of the two representations will result in a hybrid model. The input to a model will include parameters that define the computer system being modeled and the workload. The model output should include the performance measures of interest such as response time, turnaround time, throughput, and utilization. The objective of modeling is to enable the prediction of system behaviors under various circumstances which are defined by the parameters input to the model. A common circumstance to be studied is the increased workload. The model output will identify the level of workload which can cause the system performance to become unacceptable, and which component is the cause of bottleneck. Other circumstances to be studied include significant software changes and technological developments that may cause substantial changes in workload patterns. The model can be modified to reflect these changes and the output can be defined to provide the rquired information. With this kind of insight, capacity planners will then be in a position to plan what and when changes to the existing facilities need to be made.

An approach that is especially suitable for modeling computer systems is the queueing network modeling. As discussed in Chapter 2, a queueing network model represents a computer system as a network of queues. Each queue is associated with a service center which represents a system resource (e.g., CPU, disk) being competed for use by user transactions and user jobs. Under this model, a job exiting from a service center will become input to other service centers. The job will route through a number of service centers in a manner as specified in the model parameters, and then exit the system as it finishes. This description corresponds closely to job execution in actual computer systems. The complexity of the model can be controlled by specifying the number and types of service centers, routing characteristics, and the number of workload classes.

The appropriateness of queueing network modeling as a tool for computer capacity planning is due to its relatively accurate predictions at relatively low cost. From the reported experiences on the applications of queueing network models, the results are typically accurate to within 5 to 10% for utilization and 10 to 30% for response time predictions [See, for example, Lipsky and Church 1977, Lo 1980, and Sanguinette and Billington 1980]. The relatively low cost of the approach is obvious when compared to the simulation approach: there is no complex program to write and debug, and no lengthy program to execute. Furthermore, the definition of a queueing network model is relatively straightforward due to the close correspondence between the attributes of queueing network models and the attributes of computer systems, as discussed above. Parameters required as input to the model can be obtained readily from measurement data given by most hardware, software, and resource accounting monitors. The recent developments of the operational analysis approach of queueing network modeling have made the model assumptions to be more easily tested and understood [Denning and Buzen 1978, Lazowska et al. 1984]. And finally, computations required to produce the model output are enhanced by the development of fast exact and approximate algorithms therefore efficiency of the approach is greatly improved [Denning and Buzen 1978, Sauer and Chandy 1980, Chandy and Neuse 1982].

Where the system is very complex, the system behavior violates major assumptions of the queueing network model, or the information being sought is much more detailed than a queueing network model can provide, then simulation modeling can be employed. When the expense of simulation is prohibitive and the queueing network modeling is inadequate, then hybrid modeling can be used to take advantage of both approaches: the efficiency of queueing network modeling and the capability for details of simulation modeling.

In order to predict future workload, a model must also be constructed based on historical workload and perhaps other data. Common forecasting models that can be applied to workload forecasting include time series regression models, structural models, Box-Jenkins models, technological forecasting models, as discussed in Chapter 2. The projected workload as obtained from the selected forecasting model will be used as the input parameters to the system model for the prediction of performance under future workload. The predicted performance measures will then provide a direct indication of the need for configuration changes, if any, and what and when the changes should be made. The system model may also be constructed so that proposed changes to the existing system can be reflected, thus expected performance on "new" systems under different proposals can be compared and evaluated.

In the remainder of this section, we will present a procedure for capacity study based on queueing network modeling, an example applying the procedure, and an evaluation of the strengths and weaknesses of the procedure.

3.3.2 A Capacity Study Procedure -- System Modeling Approach

A capacity study based on queueing network modeling will involve the following steps. These steps will be elaborated upon later.

(1) Obtain a clear description of the system from the system inventory, giving the major resources (CPU, disks, etc.) in the system and their characteristics (CPU speed, disk data transfer rate, etc.)

(2) Identify workload components and obtain measurement data regarding each workload component.

(3) Forecast the rate of growth for each workload component.

(4) Construct a queueing network model based on the workload and system description as obtained above. For reasons that will be discussed later, some workload components may be combined to form a workload class as defined in the queueing network model.

(5) Calculate performance measures from the model, with model parameters defined from measurement data obtained in a selected observation period.

(6) Validate the model by comparing the calculated performance quantities with their measured counterparts from the observation period. Proceed to the next step only after the model is validated.

(7) With the validated model, predict the performance of each workload class under the projected future workload. The predicted performance measures at different levels of projected workload will enable the identification of when and what needs to be upgraded.

(8) Examine the various alternatives for system changes that can be used to avoid the performance degradation as identified in the performance prediction step. Alternative proposals may be analyzed by modifying the queueing network model to reflect the proposed changes. The model outputs will be extremely useful in the technical and financial evaluation of the alternatives.

Each of the above steps will be explained in more detail in the following subsections. It should be noted that the same selection and acquisition process as discussed in the component approach is also required here after the proposal for upgrade has been approved by appropriate levels of management. As stated earlier, with significant improvements on price/performance ratios in new technology, installations may find it beneficial to upgrade its computer facilities even prior to system overload. Therefore, if the capacity study is initiated due to technological advances, and the performance objectives are not expected to exceed the thresholds within the forecast period, a cost and benefits analysis of the upgrade alternative should be carried out before a potentially beneficial upgrade can be ruled out.

3.3.3 Describing the System

The basis of modeling is a thorough understanding of the system being modeled. The system inventory should provide a clear description of the system, listing the system resources, their theoretical capacity and capability (as provided by the manufacturers), and how they are interconnected. Other information such as how a job arriving at a resource center gets serviced (whether queueing is required, what queueing discipline is used: first in first out, priority, etc.) should also be specified. For the purpose of modeling, only the points of potential congestion or delay within the part of the system under study need to be represented. For example, unit record equipment such as printers can be ignored unless we are specifically studying the spooling subsystem.

3.3.4 Describing the Workload

Most large computer installation have several identifiable workload components, typically including an interactive, one or more transaction processing, and one or more batch components. In general, each workload component consists of job requests with similar service demands on the system resources. For example, an installation may find that its workload consists of an interactive service, a database service, a data entry service, a day time demand batch service, and an overnight batch service mainly for production jobs. The interactive service is broken down into day time and night time load so that the total workload is divided into two shifts: the day shift consisting of the day time interactive, the demand batch, the database, and the data entry services; and the night shift consisting of the night time interactive and the production batch services.   If the two shifts have minimum overlapping, they can be treated as if they were on two separate systems and thus can be studied separately.

Data to be collected regarding each workload component will include its volume and its characteristics. The volume of workload for the interactive service can typically be measured by the number of terminal users simultaneously logged on to the system and the average time terminal users spent on deciding and entering an interactive command (user think time). For batch service the volume can be measured by the number of batch jobs required to be executed in a given time period, or required throughput. For transaction processing service the volume can be measured by the rate of arrival of the transaction requests. The actual load of these jobs and transactions to the system depends on many more factors, namely, the characteristics of the workload. Measurement data are required to perform the workload characterization. The exact workload characterizaiton parameters required for input to the queueing network model can only be determined after the model is defined and the service centers in the model selected. However, a high level, machine independent charaterization can be made at this point giving, for example, the relative significance of the workload components, and what is involved to service a request in each component (e.g., average program size, computation or I/O bound, average number of files accessed, average file size).

3.3.5 Forecasting the Workload

The forecasting of workload measures required in queueing network models includes the volume and the characteristics of each workload component. One consideration in the identification of workload components is whether the grouping of jobs into a component allows natural forecasting. For example, production batch jobs and terminal interactive workload do not mix well since they do not normally grow in the same way. It is common that production batch jobs grow in size due to business expansion but do not grow fast in number, whereas terminal users simultaneously logged on to the system tend to grow in number but the average request job size may be quite stable.

Quantities to be forecasted should include:

(1)   For interactive service

   . N, number of terminal users simultaneously logged on

   . Z, user think time

   . S, job size

(2)   For batch service

   . X, number of batch jobs that need to be completed in a given
      time interval

   . S, job size

(3)   For transaction service

   . A, number of transactions arrived in a given time interval

   . S, transaction job size

These data are to be collected from measurement data. All forecasting
methods require historical data for a sufficient length of time. Since
queueing network modeling deals mainly with average system bahavior, the
workload measures to be forecasted are also average values. For
instance, we may obtain the average during the day shift and the average
during peak period (e.g., 9:30-11:30 a.m., and 1:30-3:30 p.m.) for N, Z,
and S in the interactive service and similar measures in other services.
The job size, S, may need several quantities to represent including CPU
execution time, I/O counts, data bytes transferred, memory residency,
and so on. It is a normal expectation that user think time and interactive job size do not change much over time, unless the system is in a
transition period (e.g., users change from a training status to becoming
proficient) or there is a major change in software (e.g., the editor is
changed from line editing mode to screen editing mode). The careful

capacity planner should verify whether changes did or are expected to take place from the measurement data as well as from the personnel involved in system software management.

The projection of N can be done using one of the forecasting methods discussed in Chapter 2. For example, we may use the moving averages model with the weekly averages of the peak period N value over the past 2 years to forecast the same. The Box-Jenkins method, or a structural model may also be used. To identify a structural model for the number of simultaneous terminal users, we first consider the factors that will have potential effects on the number. The likely candidate factors include: the number of installed terminals, the number of users given accounts to use interactive service, and the number of applications that can be accessed through the interactive service (e.g., word processing, financial analysis, simulation). Historical data on N and all potential factors must be collected. Statistical analysis is employed to select factors which do exhibit significant influence on N, and to determine the relationship between N and the significant factors. Regression is a common method for this type of analysis. Most commercial statistical packages have software routines to perform Box-Jenkins, regression, and other similar analysis. See, for example, SAS [1985] and LISREL [Joreskogand and Sorbom, 1981].

The workload measures specified for batch service are X, the required throughput, and S, the batch job size. For production batch in an established computer installation, the throughput requirement is likely to be stable. However, the job size of the production runs may change due to many factors. For example, a customer billing program will run longer as the number of customers increases. The job size in terms of CPU utilization and I/O counts has been forecasted successfully using structural models relating the job size indicators (CPU Utilization, I/O count) and key volume indicators (e.g., number of invoices, number of updates) [Sarna 1979]. How stable is the throughput requirement for production batch can be found out from measurement data and applications development personnel.

For demand batch the situation may be quite different. As the number of users and the number of application software grow, the number of batch jobs submitted by the users will increase. The upward trend on the demand batch throughput requirement is a norm rather than an exception in most organizations. Time series analysis or structural models may be used to forecast this quantity. The job sizes of demand batch however do not necessarily increase. This can be verified by statistically testing the average demand batch job sizes over the measurement periods in question.

The workload measures specified for transaction service are A, the transaction arrival rate, and S, the job size. These measures are similar to those for the demand batch service, and therefore can be forecasted similarly. Transaction processing systems are usually designed to be used by terminal users, adequate response time must therefore be maintained. As a result, transactions are generally designed with a size limitation in mind, giving another basis for the assumption of stable job size.

3.3.6 Constructing the Model

Based on the scope of the capacity study (i.e., which part of the system is to be studied), the performance measurement data (i.e., where the potential congestion point may be), the workload description (i.e., workload components and workload characteristics), and feedback from users (i.e., which workload component is most complained about, where are the likely bottlenecks in the system), an initial queueing network model can be constructed. Elements to be defined in a queueing network model include:

(1) Service centers

(2) Workload classes

(3) Workload volume for each class

(4) Service demand for each workload class on each service center.

Service Centers

The service centers of a queueing network model represent system resources where congestion or delay may result. There are many ways this representation can be made. Lazowska et al. [1984] suggested the following guidelines:

. Uniprocessor and tightly-coupled multiprocessors may be represented by a single service center. One service center may be used to represent each processor in a loosely-coupled multiprocessor system.

. Front-end communications controllers and back-end database machines may be represented as separate service centers.

. Each disk may be represented by a service center. Delay due to other I/O subsystem components (e.g., channels) is represented in the model by calculating an appropriate effective service demand for each disk.   The effective service demand is the sum of the service demand on the disk alone and a quantity that represents the average delay on the channel.

. The entire group of tape drives on a channel may be represented by a single service center.   Individual tape drives are ignored and the service demands at this service center are determined based on the utilization measurements on the channel.

. Unit record equipment such as printers may be ignored unless the study is specifically for the spooling subsystem.

. Terminal controllers are also typically ignored unless the study is to investigate specifically the delays due to the communication network including the lines and the terminal controllers.   In this case the modeling may employ the decomposition technique where the solution involves two steps: (i) solve the central subsystem model which represents all resources beyond the front-end communications controller, and (ii) construct a high-level model which includes service centers that represent components on the communication network, as well as a service center that represents the central subsystem.

The above guidelines are established based on the way equipment operates.   For example, a tape drive is not capable of operation independent of the channel, thus we can view the channel and all its connecting tape drives as a single unit.   On the other hand, disk drives are capable of performing a seek operation with minimal channel involvement. Some disks (e.g., IBM 3330 and 3350) do not require the channel to be connected even during rotational latency. Since the seek time constitutes a large portion of each disk service time, we consider the disks to be capable of (largely) parallel operations. Consequently, each disk is typically represented as a service center.

Workload Classes

The second element to be defined in a queueing network model is the workload classes which correspond closely to the workload components discussed above. A workload component must be represented as a class in the model if performance predictions for that component are desired. On the other hand, if only certain workload components' performance measures are of interest, then all other components can be aggregated into one class so as to simplify the model. Consider again the system with an interactive service, a demand batch service, a database service and a data entry service. Suppose we are only interested in the response time for the interactive service, then we can have one workload class representing the interactive component and a second class representing the rest.

On the other hand, workload classes are not limited to a small number. For example, an installation may have several batch services: one for short jobs with small memory region, one for medium size jobs with at most two tape mounts, and one for all others. Each batch service can be represented as a workload class in the model. Different applications run under the same transaction processing system can also be represented as independent classes (e.g., one class for insurance claim transactions, another class for new insurance policy underwriting transactions). The definition of workload classes is however limited by the availability of measurement data that allow reasonably accurate workload forecasts, and by the efficiency requirement in the computation of the model output.

Workload Volume

The volume of each workload class is normally set up as an input parameter to the model so that model output may be obtained for various projected workload levels. Two categories of workload classes can be defined in a queueing network model : open and closed. In an open class workload, the arrival rate of work in the class is specified as an input parameter to the model giving the workload volume. The important characteristic of an open class workload is that the arrival rate is determined by factors external to the central computer system, and that this arrival rate is known to the capacity planner. This characteristic makes the open class especially suitable for workload whose growth can be forecasted in terms of an increased arrival rate. Transaction processing services in most installations fall into this category. These services are typically set up to support business operations in the organization (e.g., insurance policy underwriting and bank account withdrawal). The growth of transaction arrival rate is therefore a function of the growth in the particular business operation the transaction processing service supports, and can be projected based on business forecasts.

A closed class workload best describes interactive services where a finite number of users are logged in to the system at the terminals. The users at the terminals generate transactions by issuing commands. Transactions arrive at the system for execution. When the execution of a transaction is completed, a response is sent to the user's terminal. The user then generates a new transactions, and the cycle is repeated. The input for the workload volume of a closed class workload includes the number of terminals simultaneously logged in, and the user think time.

A batch workload can be represented as an open class with throughput specified as the workload volume. In a system where batch processing operates under a "backlog", the batch workload is represented as a closed class. Batch jobs entering a backlogged system must wait in a queue. The system will initiate the next waiting job as long as there is enough memory space available and the number of active jobs does not exceed a predefined multiprogramming level. In a backlog situation, there is always one job waiting to be initiated. Such a situation is commonly observed during peak-hour operations. Under this circumstance, an active job after completing execution is immediately "replaced" by a new job waiting in the queue, thus forming a closed cycle. The workload volume of a batch workload with backlog is specified by the average number of active jobs in the system.

Service Demands

The last set of parameters to be specified in a queueing network model is the service demands of each workload class on each service center. This includes the number of requests, $V_{c,i}$, that a job in class c sends to service center i (also called visit ratio), and the mean service time, $S_{c,i}$, for each request. The service demand by each job of class c on center i is then

$$D_{c,i} = V_{c,i} \, S_{c,i} \qquad\qquad (3.1)$$

For example, if a database workload (class DB) accesses the disk 10 times on the average and each access takes 0.2 seconds, then we have

$$V_{DB,DISK} = 10$$
$$S_{DB,DISK} = 0.2 \text{ seconds} \qquad\qquad (3.2)$$
and
$$D_{DB,DISK} = V_{DB,DISK} \, S_{DB,DISK}$$
$$= 2 \text{ seconds.}$$

Measurement data are required to estimate service demands. The following considerations should be noted:

. Sufficient data should be used that give a representative sample of the actual demands.

. Most accounting monitors that report CPU usage by workload components do not include the operating system overhead. This overhead must be distributed to all the workload components equitably. Different distribution methods may have to be applied and evaluated. The method that results in consistent performance outputs with data from different measurement periods should be adopted.

. For disk service centers with channels not explicitly represented, the service time must be adjusted by the contention time on the channel. At the completion of a seek to the desired cylinder, the disk is held while waiting for channel to become free. This waiting is said to be due to contention and must be estimated and attributed to the appropriate disk, resulting in an effective disk service time.

. The number of I/O requests, $V_{c,i}$, in a queueing network model refers to the physical I/O. Most accounting monitors report logical I/O by job and other monitoring systems report physical I/O by device. A reasonable estimation is obtained by apportioning the total number of physical I/O on a given I/O device by the percentage of logical I/O issued by each workload class.

3.3.7 Evaluating Performance Measures

The following performance measures may be calculated from a queueing network model:

(1) For each workload class:

    . Average response time

    . Throughput

    . Average number of jobs in system.

(2) For each service center:

    . Utilization of the center

    . Average residence time at the center

    . Throughput at the center

    . Average number of jobs at the center

Different algorithms are available for solving open, closed, and mixed models. Solution techniques for multiple workload class models are basically extensions of those for the single-class models. Complex systems may be solved by first identifying subsystems that may be solved using simple queueing network models, and then constructing a high-level model composed of these subsystems. Detailed behavior of these subsystems are hidden in the high-level model; only the measures as obtained from the models of these subsystems are used.

Comprehensive treatment of the various evaluation procedures for different queueing network models can be found in Baskett et al. [1975], a special issue on queueing network models in ACM Computing Surveys [1978], and Lazowska et al. [1984]. An example will be given later in this chapter to illustrate the performance measures that can be obtained from a queueing network model.

3.3.8 Validating the Model

A model must be validated before we shall proceed with the prediction of performance. A validation procedure consists of experimentation with the model using measurement data from a variety of different observation periods. If the model outputs from each experiment compare well with their measured counterparts obtained from the corresponding observation period, then the model is considered validated.

Suppose, on the other hand, that the calculated performance quantities from the model and the measured quantities are inconsistent, or they agree at times but not at others. Then the model's predicting power may be too weak to be useful, therefore it needs to be revised. Statistical confidence tests can be used to determine if the calculated and the measured quantities are significantly different. Revising the estimation of service demands is a common area which likely leads to improved models. Other modifications may be needed, however, including changes in service center definition as well as workload classification.

3.3.9 Predicting Performance

To obtain input for workload parameters for performance prediction, the projected future workload for each workload component must be translated into workload volume and service demands. These workload parameters can be calculated with the workload projected at several intervals (e.g., quarterly) during the forecasting period. With these workload parameters as input, the model outputs will then provide the capacity planner with relatively detailed information about system behaviors in the future. Comparing these predicted performance measures over time against the performance objective for each workload class, the approximate point in time when performance becomes unacceptable can be identified. And that point in time is when an upgrade to the existing system is expected to become necessary. The detailed performance measures output from the queueing network model also allows the identification of bottleneck service centers, thereby indicating the resources that need to be upgraded.

3.3.10 Examining Alternatives

With the identification of resources that may become bottlenecks in the system's future operations and the approximate timing that this will occur, an upgrade plan of these resources can be in order. All alternative upgrade options may be analyzed by modifying the queueing network model to reflect the proposed changes.

As discussed in the component approach, any capacity study concluding with an upgrade plan assumes that the system is well tuned. If significant improvements on system performance can be achieved through tuning with justifiable effort, then the upgrade can be delayed. To prevent unnecessary upgrade, therefore, an added measure should be made by mandating the inclusion of a tuning alternative in all proposals for system changes. The advantage of using queueing network models in capacity study is that a tuning alternative can also be analyzed using the same methodology as the upgrade alternatives. Any recommended tuning action such as moving workload, reallocating files, and so on, can be represented in a queueing network model by defining the appropriate parameters to reflect the changes. Hence the evaluation of alternatives is based on comparable performance measures obtained using a unified methodology. It should be noted that a redesign of the queueing network model for the tuning option may require further data collection and parameter specification.

The next subsection provides an example to illustrate the application of queueing network modeling.

3.3.11 An Example

The example given below illustrates how queueing network modeling may be applied in computer capacity planning. It corresponds to the example system discussed earlier with four workload components for its day shift operations: a database service, a data entry service, an interactive service and a demand batch service. The model is contructed with two service centers: CPU and DISK. Queueing network models are capable of representing a large number of system resources by service centers. The considerations for the choice of service centers include: (i) usefulness of the information provided by the explicit representation of the system resource, (ii) efficiency in the computation of model output, and (iii) availability of data required for the system resources to be explicitly represented in the model.

The presentation of the example includes the input and output of the model with a high level description of the computation procedure for the output performance measures. Detailed formulae used in the computation will be collectively presented in a table. For a comprehensive discussion of algorithms for the evaluation of queueing network models, see Lazowska et al. [1984].

In studying this example one should note that there is a large amount of output performance measures, and that most performance measures are affected by a change in a single input parameter. This phenomenon is reflective of real computer systems indicating that, when used properly, queueing network models can provide significant insight into the interdependent behaviors of the real system being modeled.

System characteristics

The system being considered is a multiprogrammed system with a single CPU and a disk subsystem. As all file allocation is controlled by the operating system (i.e., user does not specify where a file is stored), individual disks in the disk subsystem are indistinguishable to the users.

Workload characteristics

The system has two shifts: the day shift consisting of a database service, a data entry service, an interactive service, and a demand batch service; and the night shift consisting of an interactive service and an overnight batch service for production jobs. The day shift load is by far the dominating load and is growing. The study will therefore concentrate on the day shift workloads.

Both the database and the data entry services are of the transaction processing type and are the more dominant workloads within this particular system. The current measurement shows the following volume of workload for these two components:

. Database   : 3600 transactions per hour

. Data entry : 1800 transactions per hour

The other two components are relatively insignificant compared to the database and the data entry services. The measurement gives the following volume:

. Interactive: 3 online users

                   25 seconds user think time

                   385 transactions per hour

. Batch   : 2 active jobs

                   216 jobs per hour.

We identify the current workload volume as W_0.

Workload Forecasting

Two situations will be considered here:

(1) The system shows steady growth and no large applications are expected to be implemented within the next four quarters. We label the workload volume projected under this scenario as W_1.

(2) A large database application is planned to be installed in one year. The existing workload is assumed to remain unchanged from the current level. The reason for this assumption is to illustrate how a single change in one component can affect the performance measures of all workloads in the entire system. We label the workload volume projected under this scenario as W_2.

With the steady growth pattern assumed in the first situation and no external factors are expected to cause abrupt change in this pattern within the forecast horizon, an autogressive regression model may be used. The quantities to be forecasted for the different components are:

. Database: transaction rate

. Data entry: transaction rate

. Interactive: number of online users

. Batch: number of active jobs.

Batch processing in this system operates under backlog. The batch workload volume is therefore specified by the number of active jobs instead of throughput. The forecasts should be made at several points in time (e.g., quarterly) within the forecast horizon. The results can be plotted in a graph as in Figure 3.3. The symbols 1Q, 2Q, 3Q, and 4Q used in the figure indicate the time points at the first, second, third, and fourth quarter, respectively, from the present.

User think time and job sizes are assumed to be unchanged which may be verified from monitored data.

For the second situation the volume of the new application must be estimated. Through analyses of the structure, the operations involved, the dependency on input data, and the input and output file sizes of new application, similar transactions from the existing applications are identified. Measurements on these existing transactions are then used as the basis for estimating the volume and transaction job size of the new application. Since the objective of this illustration is to show how a single change can affect the entire system, we assume that the new transactions are similar to the existing ones thus making the average job size in the database component unchanged. The new addition however will cause a 30% increase of transaction rate for the database service.

Figure 3.3

WORKLOAD FORECASTS ASSUMING STEADY GROWTH

(a) TRANSACTION SERVICES

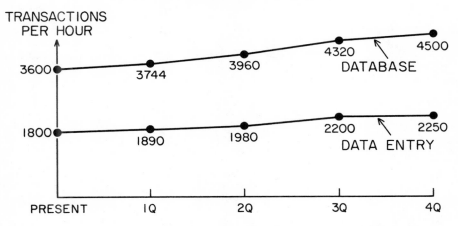

(b) INTERACTIVE AND BATCH SERVICES

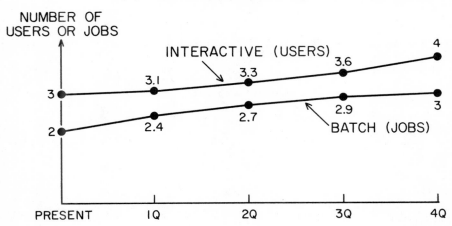

The Model

Based on the system and workload characteristics we can now define a queueing network model as depicted in Figure 3.4. The model consists of two service centers: CPU and DISK. Three workload classes are defined: DB for the database component, DE for the data entry component and COM for the combined interactive and batch components. The rationale here is that the two latter components are small in comparison with the database and data entry components. For this particular capacity study there is no real need for reporting performance measures separately for them. The combined workload is treated as a closed workload class with parameters defined from measurement data for the two components. Table 3.1 shows the measurement data for the interactive and batch components from an observation period, and the corresponding quantities for the combined workload class calculated from these data. Similar measured quantities required as input to the model for the database and the data entry classes are shown in Table 3.2.

The model being defined is a mixed model since it consists of two open workload classes representing the two transaction services, and one closed class representing the combined interactive and batch components. With the model set up and all workload parameters specified, we can now proceed to calculate the output performance measures from the model.

Performance Evaluation and Prediction

The model will be solved using an algorithm for mixed queueing net-work models as given in Lazowska [1984, p. 146]. The algorithm is summarized below. Formulae needed in the algorithm are included in

Figure 3.4

A QUEUEING NETWORK MODEL
FOR THREE WORKLOAD CLASSES

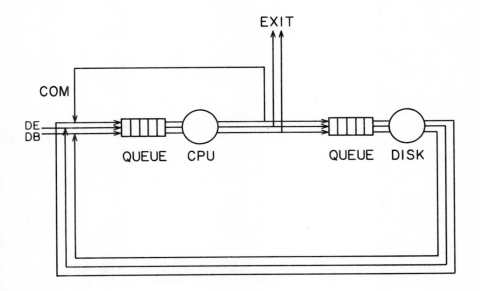

TABLE 3.1

COMBINING INTERACTIVE AND BATCH COMPONENTS INTO ONE CLASS

Measured Quantity	Interactive	Batch	Combined
Job completion count (C)	385.00	216.00	601.00*
Number of active users/jobs (N)	3.00	2.00	5.00*
User think time in seconds (Z)	23.40	0.00	15.00**
Device busy in seconds (B)			
CPU	200.00	401.00	601.00*
DISK	680.00	522.00	1,202.00*
Service demands in seconds per transaction (D=B/C)			
CPU	0.52	1.86	1.00
DISK	1.77	2.42	2.00
Device visit count (K)			
CPU	36340.00	23760.00	60100.00*
DISK	18780.00	17280.00	36060.00*
Device visit ratio (V=K/C)			
CPU	94.39	110.00	100.00
DISK	48.78	80.00	60.00

* These quantities are obtained by adding the two corresponding quantities for the interactive and batch services. For example, the job completion count for the combined workload class is 385.00 + 216.00 = 601.00.

** The user think time for the combined workload class is the weighted average of the user think times for the interactive and batch services, i.e., (23.40 X 385 + 0 X 216)/601 = 15.00.

TABLE 3.2

MEASUREMENT FOR THE DATABASE AND DATA ENTRY WORKLOAD CLASSES

Measured Quantity	Database (DB)	Data Entry (DE)
Length of observation period in seconds (T)	3600.0	3600.0
Transaction completion count (C)	3600.0	1800.0
Transaction rate (A=C/T)	1.0	0.5
Device busy in seconds (B) CPU	1080.0	900.0
DISK	1800.0	360.0
Service demand in seconds per transaction (D=B/C) CPU	0.3	0.5
DISK	0.5	0.2
Device visit count (K) CPU	108000.0	72000.0
DISK	180000.0	36000.0
Device visit ratio (V=K/C) CPU	30.0	40.0
DISK	50.0	20.0

Table 3.3 for the convenience of the interested reader. Detailed derivation and explanations of these formulae are beyond the scope of this book, and can be found in Lazowska [1984, pp. 134-148 and pp. 112-117].

(1) Obtain the throughput of all open class workloads, in this case DB and DE (X_{DB}, X_{DE}, $X_{DB,CPU}$, $X_{DB,DISK}$, $X_{DE,CPU}$ and $X_{DE,DISK}$), using equations (3.3) and (3.4) in Table 3.3.

(2) Compute the utilization of all service centers (CPU and DISK in this model) due to each open class ($U_{DB,CPU}$, $U_{DB,DISK}$, $U_{DE,CPU}$ and $U_{DE,DISK}$) and all open classes together ($U_{\{DB,DE\},CPU}$ and $U_{\{DB,DE\},DISK}$), using equations (3.5) and (3.6).

(3) Assume the open class workloads (DB and DE) are deleted from the model thereby resulting in a closed queueing network model. The remaining capacity of a service center i after reducing the amount taken up by all the open class workloads will be ($1 - U_{\{DB,DE\},i}$). The service demand of the closed class workload (COM) on a service center i with reduced capacity ($1 - U_{\{DB,DE\},i}$) will be increased by a factor of $1/(1 - U_{\{DB,DE\},i})$. Therefore we obtain "inflated" service demands ($D^{*}_{COM,CPU}$ and $D^{*}_{COM,DISK}$) for the closed class workload (COM) on service centers CPU and DISK as in equation (3.7).

(4) Solve the closed model with the "inflated" service demands. Obtain the following performance quantities, first by an iterative procedure applying equations (3.8) to (3.10) and then using equations (3.11) to (3.14).

TABLE 3.3

NOTATIONS AND FORMULAE
FOR A MIXED QUEUEING NETWORK MODEL

(a) Notation

c = workload class (DB, DE, or COM)

i = service center (CPU or DISK)

N = number of interactive and batch jobs in the system (for the COM class, known from Table 3.1)

Z = user think time (known from Table 3.1)

A_c = arrival rate of workload class c (known from Table 3.2)

X_c = system throughput for workload class c

R_c = system response time for workload class c

Q_c = number of jobs in system for workload class c

U_i = utilization of service center i

$X_{c,i}$ = throughput at service center i for workload class c

$V_{c,i}$ = visit ratio of workload class c to service center i

$D_{c,i}$ = service demand of workload class c on service center i (known from Tables 3.1 and 3.2)

$D^*_{c,i}$ = "inflated" service demand of workload class c on service center i with reduced capacity

$U_{c,i}$ = utilization of service center i due to workload class c

$U_{\{O\},i}$ = utilization of service center i due to all open workload classes

$R_{c,i}$ = residence time of workload class c in service center i

$Q_{c,i}$ = queue length of workload class c in service center i

$Q_{\{C\},i}$ = total queue length of all closed workload classes at service center i.

TABLE 3.3 (Cont'd.)

(b) <u>Formulae</u>

(1)   Throughput for open workload classes

$$X_c = A_c \qquad\qquad (3.3)$$

$$X_{c,i} = X_c\, V_{c,i} \qquad\qquad (3.4)$$

(2)   Utilization for open workload classes

$$U_{c,i} = X_c\, D_{c,i} \qquad\qquad (3.5)$$

$$U_{\{O\},i} = \sum_{c \text{ in } \{O\}} U_{c,i} \qquad\qquad (3.6)$$

(3)   "Inflated" service demand for closed workload class

$$D^*_{c,i} = \frac{D_{c,i}}{1 - U_{\{O\},i}} \qquad\qquad (3.7)$$

(4)   Throughput, residence time and queue length for closed workload class are obtained by an iterative procedure. The folowing procedure is given for a single closed class c.

(i)   Set $Q_{c,i} = 0$ for each service center i.

(ii)   Repeat the following computations N times, each time using the most recent values of $Q_{c,i}$, $R_{c,i}$ and X_c.

$$R_{c,i} = D^*_{c,i}\,(1 + Q_{c,i}) \text{ for each i} \qquad\qquad (3.8)$$

$$X_c = \frac{N}{Z + \sum_{\text{all } i} R_{c,i}} \qquad\qquad (3.9)$$

$$Q_{c,i} = X_c\, R_{c,i} \text{ for each i.} \qquad\qquad (3.10)$$

TABLE 3.3 (Cont'd.)

(iii) Using the final values of $Q_{c,i}$ and $R_{c,i}$ obtained in (ii), compute

$$R_c = \sum_{\text{all } i} R_{c,i} \tag{3.11}$$

and

$$Q_c = \sum_{\text{all } i} Q_{c,i} \tag{3.12}$$

(iv) Using the final values of X_c obtained in (ii), compute

$$X_{c,i} = X_c V_{c,i} \tag{3.13}$$

and

$$U_{c,i} = X_c D_{c,i} \tag{3.14}$$

(5) Residence time and queue length for open workload class c

$$R_{c,i} = \frac{D_{c,i} (1 + Q_{\{C\},i})}{1 - U_{\{O\},i}} \tag{3.15}$$

$$Q_{c,i} = X_c R_{c,i} \tag{3.16}$$

$$R_c = \sum_{\text{all } i} R_{c,i} \tag{3.17}$$

$$Q_c = \sum_{\text{all } i} Q_{c,i} \tag{3.18}$$

For the system:

- Throughput (X_{COM})
- Average response time (R_{COM})
- Number of jobs in the system (Q_{COM})

For each service center:

- Throughput $(X_{COM,CPU}$ and $X_{COM,DISK})$
- Utilization $(U_{COM,CPU}$ and $U_{COM,DISK})$
- Average residence time $(R_{COM,CPU}$ and $R_{COM,DISK}$, total time spent at the center by a job)
- Average queue length $(Q_{COM,CPU}$ and $Q_{COM,DISK}$, includes the job being processed).

(5)   Compute the remaining performance measures for each open class workload (DB and DE here), using equations (3.15) to (3.18). These include :

For the system:

- Average response time (R_{DB}, R_{DE})
- Number of jobs in system (Q_{DB}, Q_{DE})

For each service center:

- Average residence time $(R_{DB,CPU}, R_{DB,DISK}, R_{DE,CPU}, R_{DE,DISK})$
- Average queue length $(Q_{DB,CPU}, Q_{DB,DISK}, Q_{DE,CPU}, Q_{DE,DISK})$.

The performance quantities calculated for the current workload will be compared to their measured counterpart. Only after the model validation is satisfied shall we proceed with the performance prediction step.

Table 3.4 shows the performance measures obtained from this model for the current workload (W_0), for a forecasted workload at the 2nd quarter (W_1) as given in Figure 3.3, and for a forecasted 30% increase in DB workload volume due to the new database application (W_2). The throughput is reported in number of jobs per second, and the response times and residence times are in seconds.

The results given in Table 3.4 indicate two important points:

(1)   A change in the volume of a single workload component can change almost all performance measures in the system, some by a very wide margin. For example, the response times of the DB and COM classes are almost doubled when workload volume is changed from W_0 to W_2.

(2)   The device utilization by individual workload class has very little bearing on the system-wide response time for that class. For example, with 30% increase of the DB load, the CPU utilization by the DB class is only increased from 0.30 to 0.39, and the utilization by the COM class has even decreased. However, the response times for both classes have almost doubled.

Performance measures such as those reported in Table 3.4 allow a capacity planner to conclude if the system has adequate capacity to support the increased workload as forecasted. Suppose the performance objective has been established that a 5-second average response time is required for transaction processing, then the results indicate that the current setting will be inadequate at W_1 or W_2. Either some work has to be moved to the night shift, or capacity needs to be upgraded. From Table 3.4, the total utilization of the CPU is 0.77 and that of the disk

TABLE 3.4

PERFORMANCE MEASURES CALCULATED FROM
THE QUEUEING NETWORK MODEL

Workload Class	Performance Quantity	Current Workload W_0	Steady Growth Forecast at 2nd Quarter W_1	30% Increase in DB W_2
DB	System-wide:			
	Throughput X	1.00	1.10	1.30
	Response Time R	4.75	7.12	8.79
	Number in system Q	4.75	7.83	11.43
	Center CPU:			
	Throughput X	30.00	33.00	39.00
	Utilization U	0.30	0.33	0.39
	Residence time R	1.02	1.23	1.21
	Queue length Q	1.02	1.35	1.57
	Center DISK:			
	Throughput X	50.00	55.00	65.00
	Utilization U	0.50	0.55	0.65
	Residence time R	3.73	5.89	7.58
	Queue length Q	3.73	6.48	9.85
DE	System-wide:			
	Throughput X	0.50	0.55	0.50
	Response time R	3.19	4.61	5.05
	Number in system Q	1.60	2.54	2.53
	Center CPU:			
	Throughput X	20.00	22.00	20.00
	Utilization U	0.25	0.28	0.25
	Residence time R	1.70	2.25	2.02
	Queue length Q	0.85	1.24	1.01
	Center DISK:			
	Throughput X	10.00	11.00	10.00
	Utilization U	0.10	0.11	0.10
	Residence time R	1.49	2.36	3.03
	Queue length Q	0.75	1.30	1.52
COM	System-wide:			
	Throughput X	0.17	0.16	0.12
	Response time R	15.12	22.97	27.74
	Number in system Q	2.51	2.63	3.25
	Center CPU:			
	Throughput X	16.60	15.80	11.70
	Utilization U	0.17	0.16	0.12
	Residence time R	3.17	3.90	3.88
	Queue length Q	0.53	0.62	0.45
	Center DISK:			
	Throughput X	9.96	9.48	7.02
	Utilization U	0.33	0.32	0.23
	Residence time R	11.95	19.04	23.84
	Queue length Q	1.98	3.01	2.79

is 0.98 at W_1, and the corresponding quantities at W_2 are 0.76 and 0.98. The disk system appears to be the bottleneck under the increased load. Therefore an upgrade of the disk system will be fruitful.

3.3.12 Strengths and Weaknesses

The major strengths of the system modeling approach based on queueing network models lie on the amount of detailed measures it can provide on the system being modeled, normally at a relatively low cost. Instead of limited information on individual resources as that obtained using the component approach, the system modeling approach provides information about the behavior of the entire system as represented by the model.

A second advantage of this approach is due to its versatility. Once a model has been constructed, it can be used for getting insight about the existing system under the current workload, as well as predicting performance of the existing system when workload is increased. Due to the efficiency of the evaluation procedure, various combinations of different growth rates can be attempted to allow prediction of system behaviors under different scenarios. Once the need for upgrade is predicted, the model can also be modified to reflect alternative proposed actions (include tuning and different upgrade options). Performance measures output from these models can be extremely useful for the evaluation of the various alternatives. Of course, these projected performance measures cannot be validated until the alternative is actually implemented.

A third advantage of this approach is due to recent developments of performance modeling software packages such as BEST/1 by BGS Systems [1982], MAP by Quantitative System Performance [1982], PAWS/A by Information Research Associates [1983], and PEP38 (Performance Expert Prototypes for IBM System/38) by Stroebel et al. [1986]. With the availability of these software packages, capacity planners need only a basic understanding of system modeling in order to implement capacity planning using this approach. The experiences of a number of applications of this approach indicate that relatively accurate performance prediction can be expected.

The system modeling approach is not without weaknesses, however. First, there are some underlying assumptions in queueing network modeling that may not always be satisfied in real systems. Examples include the homogeneity assumption using operational analysis [Denning and Buzen 1978] and exponential service time distribution assumption using stochastic analysis [Kleinrock 1975]. When underlying assumptions are grossly violated, poor results from the model can be expected.

Theoretically, queueing network models can be constructed to represent as many workload classes and service centers as desired. However, when the model is large, computation may become prohibitively expensive. In this case approximate solution techniques may have to be used in lieu of the exact solution. At present, error bounds from the available approximate methods are still under development even though practical experiences employing approximate methods appear to be quite satisfactory [Muntz 1978, Lazowska et al. 1984].

3.4 Summary

A successful computer capacity plan relies on a good understanding
of the computer installation's current system environment and a reliable
projection of the organization's future computing needs. Such an understanding is usually gained from a well designed capacity study which may
be launched as frequently as required. In this chapter we presented two
approaches for implementing the computer capacity planning function.
The objective of a capacity study is to identify the future point in
time when a change in the configuration is beneficial. One situation is
when system performance is expected to become unacceptable so that actions should be taken to avoid it. The capacity study should also identify possible actions. Other situations include the lease expiration of
major components, and anticipation of significant technological development that may affect the installation's workload patterns or user
requirements.

The two approaches presented are: component approach and system
modeling approach. With the component approach the various resource
components in the computer system are treated independently. Utilization of each major resource is monitored and tracked. Trends of the
utilization curves are identified and extrapolated. Projected utilization of each resource component is compared against utilization
thresholds for that type of resource which are developed based on some
rules of thumb established either from past experiences or through
industry-wide experiences. The point at which the projected utilization
exceeds the threshold is when upgrade for that component is to be called

for.

The system modeling approach takes a system point of view and a model is constructed for the system. System behavior as output from the model under projected future workload will be used as the basis for a capacity plan. The procedure presented for a capacity study is based on queueing network modeling. This modeling technique is selected because it can be implemented relatively efficiently and provides thorough information about system behavior.

This chapter discussed these two approaches in detail. It presented a procedure for carrying out a capacity study using each approach, an example applying the procedure, and an assessment of the strengths and weaknesses of each approach.

CHAPTER 4

AN EMPIRICAL STUDY OF COMPUTER CAPACITY PLANNING PRACTICES

4.1 Study Objectives

As discussed in the previous chapters, most of the publications on computer capacity planning concentrated on explaining the principles and techniques developed for the function. Not much work has been done to assess the extent these principles and techniques have been applied in practice. Two surveys have been reported giving some indications on the practices of computer capacity planning [Kelly 1983, Morino Associates 1983]. However, as mentioned in Chapter 1, these surveys are different in scope using less scientific methodologies.

It is felt that a more comprehensive survey together with a more rigorous research methodology are necessary to better assess the useful-ness of the various approaches and tools of computer capacity planning under different circumstances. This chapter and the next present the results of such a study. The study involves a questionnaire survey of the 1985 Fortune 1000 companies (Industial 500 and Service 500) [Fortune, 1985]. The Fortune 1000 companies are commonly used as the

129

population representing large corporations in America.

The results of this empirical research study are being organized into three major areas:

(1) The overall tendency of how the various aspects of computer capacity planning are being handled in practice;

(2) The computing and business environments of the respondent companies; and

(3) The effect of environmental characteristics on computer capacity planning practices.

Part (1) of the results will be presented in this chapter, and parts (2) and (3) will be discussed in the next chapter.

These results should be of interest to researchers to assess the future direction of research in computer capacity planning as they provide insight into the degree of applicability of the various theories and techniques and what is in need in the real world. These results should also provide guidance to data processing analysts and managers who are faced with the practical reality of computer capacity planning by broadening their understanding of how other companies carry out this function and what environmental factors can significantly affect practices. Equipment manufacturers and software developers should find these results useful as they provide direct consumer information that can help guide the development of their new machines or new software packages. Finally, internal and external auditors may also enhance the quality of their management advisory services by gaining insight on how to measure, evaluate and improve the performance of their own or their clients' computer facilities.

In the next section, five critical issues in the practice of computer capacity planning and the design of the questionnaire will be discussed. The survey methodology, the distributions of the questionnaire and the responses will be presented in Section 4.3. Section 4.4 will detail the overall rating results of the survey and Section 4.5 will discuss some implications of these overall ratings. A summary of the chapter will be given in Section 4.6, followed by the Appendix showing the questionnaire used in the survey study.

4.2 Critical Practice Issues and the Questionnaire

After an extensive review of the current literature and based on the authors' personal experiences, a list of critical issues related to computer capacity planning in large corporations was constructed and included in the questionnaire. The questionnaire shown in the Appendix is the final version which was revised based on a careful review of a pilot survey. The questionnaire covers five critical issues as well as questions about the company's business and computing environments. We intended to minimize the length of this questionnaire as much as possible in order to obtain a satisfactory response rate. The five critical issues are outlined in the following five subsections. The choice of questions pertaining to the company's business and computing environments will be explained in Chapter 5.

4.2.1 Approaches Used for Computer System Analysis

There are different approaches that can be used to analyze the system behavior to determine when and what the next capacity upgrade should
be for a computer installation. Chapter 3 presented two approaches: a
component approach which considers the utilization of each component in
the system separately; and a system modeling approach which considers
the system as a whole and tries to identify bottlenecks when the system
performance is expected to fall below a predetermined objective. The
component approach has existed for a long time and relies heavily on
rules of thumb. The system modeling approach is based on the modeling
methodologies that have undergone rapid development over the past
decade. Due to the relative efficiency in its implementation, the relative accuracy of its analysis results, the versatility of its
application, and the relatively large amount of information the model
output provides, this approach is expected to become widely used.
Moreover, the development of commercial modeling packages should enhance
the acceptance of the system modeling approach.

Other approaches also exist. For example, with the rapid development in electronic technology, new products are always found to provide
much better price/performance ratio than the existing ones. As a
result, computer installations may well find it to be beneficial to time
its upgrade with the introduction of new products. For example, new
technology on data storage (e.g. optical disk) can drastically change
the way that long term data is stored, archived, as well accessed. The
announcement or anticipation of products of this kind may very well

prompt a capacity study which can result in a recommendation to acquire the new data storage system in due time. Suppose, on the other hand, workload is projected to exceed the existing CPU capacity in June, but a new, powerful CPU is expected to become available in October which will not only provide the required capacity (may be more than required) but also have a very attractive price advantage. Then, instead of planning a permanent upgrade for June, the installation may decide to plan for the new machine in October and make temporary arrangement (service bureau, short-term lease, etc.) for the time between June and October. The timing of the introduction of new products are often accompanied by large discounts of old models. Some installations therefore project the timing of new products so as to take advantage of price discounts of the old models for their upgrades. In any event, technological innovations can be an important consideration in upgrade decisions for some installations.

To assess the extent that these approaches and techniques are being used in practice, we have included three relevant questions in the questionnaire (Questions 2, 3, and 4). Questions 2 and 3 deal with CPU and disk upgrades respectively, and Question 4 deals with performance prediction. We have addressed only the CPU and disk upgrades because (i) we intend to keep the questionnaire as brief as possible to maximize the rate of response, and (ii) we believe the response given for CPU and disk alone will be indicative of the extent of the applicability of the different approaches. CPU is selected since it is the most critical and a costly computer system component [Pick 1986, p.254, Verity 1985]. Disk is selected since it is also a costly item [Pick 1986, p.254] and is widely believed to be the fastest growing component [Stamps 1985].

4.2.2 Computer Performance and User Productivity

Computer systems are installed to improve user productivity. A mandate of every computer installation is to maintain the computer system performance at a certain level so that the user's productivity will not be adversely affected. It is therefore to the advantage of every computer installation to establish a set of performance objectives as discussed in Chapter 2. These performance objectives should represent a standard of service levels the data center is committed to in offering the services to the users. They also provide the user an indication of what to expect from the system.

If properly established, performance objectives can be a very useful mechanism for the management of a computer system. Performance objectives to be established may include interactive response time, batch turnaround time, as well as system availability and reliability. The question is what values should they be set to in terms of averages and tolerance levels.

In determining the proper performance objectives, two major considerations are the effect of computer performance on user productivity, and the cost of acquiring the necessary components to achieve the required performance level. Many installations will base on past performance experience in establishing their objectives. Industry-wide practice, especially the practice of installations in the same type of industry as their own, will provide useful guidelines for establishing the objectives. The availability of data on industry-wide practice may be a problem, however. Most mainframe and minicomputer installations today consist of large networks of computer terminals that allow direct user access to the computer facilities. To get users involved has therefore been increasingly emphasized in data processing management. Many computer centers therefore go through serious discussions and negotiations with user groups to arrive at mutually agreeable service level agreement which is to become the performance objectives of the computer installation.

A more scientific method to establish the performance objectives for an installation would have to base on a careful study on the effect of computer performance on the installation's user productivity. The effect of response time on user productivity has been of great interest among researchers and practitioners. For example, a study by Thadhani [1981] has shown that, for system development work, user productivity when measured by the number of interactions with the system, grows non-linearly in the sub-second response time region. On the other hand, in the experiment by Barber and Lucas [1983] with a group of terminal operators doing complex circuit layout work, a 12-second response time appeared to be appropriate as error rate increased when response time increased or decreased from the 12-second vicinity. Other reports also discussed the appropriateness of fast response time in terms of its impact on user productivity. (See, for example, Williams and Swenson [1977], Smith [1983], and Lyman et al. [1985].) Miller's [1976] study showed that variation in response time has a significant effect on user attitude towards his or her work. A comprehensive survey on this issue can be found in Shneiderman [1984]. It is obvious that computer system performance (especially terminal response time) is widely believed to have impact on user productivity, but the levels of performance required may differ from one type of work to another. How many and what installations have conducted extensive study on their own user group's need in terms of response time would be useful information to assess the impact of the theory outlined in these studies.

Question 5 in the questionnaire is designed to find out if computer installations indeed have performance objectives established, and how the objectives are established. This, coupled with Questions 2 and 3 will also help to determine if these performance objectives are being used in computer upgrade decisions in a direct way.

4.2.3 Computer Workload Forecast

Forecasting workload is an essential element in computer capacity planning. As discussed in Chapter 2, available methods range from judgmental, seat-of-the-pants approach to highly sophisticated, scientific techniques such as the Box-Jenkins models and Delphi analysis. Some data centers also involve user departments in the forecasting process. Numerous reports on the subject of workload forecasting can be found in the literature. For example, Sarna [1979] demonstrated a structural model for forecasting the CPU and I/O usage of an accounts receivable application using the number of invoices and open-term records as the key volume indicators, and the result was found to be satisfactory. Luistro [1983] and Biasi [1985] presented some methodologies for workload forecasting, and Wandzilak [1984] discussed some common problems facing the forecasters of computer workload. Many practitioners express frustrations over the difficulties in workload forecasting [Burton 1984]. The questions of what forecasting methods are being used and how often they are used have been incorporated in the questionnaire (Question 6).

4.2.4 Computer Workload Measures

Kelly [18] reported that, from his interviews with data processing managers, it is evident that there are no definitive answers for the definition of workload or capacity. Without a proper definition, it would be difficult for capacity planners to measure properly and communicate to the management in the organization how much work is being done on the computer system and how much more work can the system handle. The traditional view of computer capacity is CPU hours, hence workload is commonly measured by the total CPU hours consumed by the computer jobs run during a given measurement period. Alternatively, CPU utilization can be computed from the measurement of CPU-hour consumption. The measurement of CPU utilization is a key workload indicator for capacity planning when the component approach is used. The level of utilization on the CPU will also help identify if CPU is the bottleneck component, when the system modeling approach is used. The advantage of this measure is that it is readily available from most hardware, software, and accounting monitors. The disadvantages include: (i) It may have little bearing on the load to other components in the

system. Therefore the data center is likely to need other workload indicators including I/O counts, communications network traffic rate,
print lines, and so on. (ii) Users are likely to find little association with it and are therefore unable to provide reliable forecast of
their future needs based on this workload measure. (iii) A conversion
on the measure is required when the installation changes from one CPU
model to another.

     Some operating systems use composite measure, such as IBM's service
units and Univac's Standard Unit of Processing (SUP) for allocation of
system resources. These composite measures are basically some weighted
sums of the utilization of critical resources such as CPU, memory, and
input/output channel. They can also be used as the units for billing.
These measures have the advantage of showing the overall workload trend
of the system in one index. The problems with their use in capacity
planning include: (i) It is difficult to establish an upper bound for
the capacity of a given computer system in terms of these composite
units. (ii) Bottleneck components cannot be identified based on the
composite measures. (iii) A conversion on the measure is required when-
ever the configuration change includes a resource whose usage is incorporated in the composite measure. Other measures such as
transaction/job counts and network load are also frequently mentioned as
indications of workload. They are required when the system modeling approach is used. Question 7 in the questionnaire was designed to assess
the extent these measures are being used in the industry.

4.2.5 System Monitoring

Proper capacity planning relies on sound knowledge of the working of the current system. This normally implies the need for the collection and analysis of data useful for evaluating the system, especially in large and complex installations. Many hardware, software, and accounting monitors are designed and have been installed for this purpose. As discussed in Chapter 2, data may be collected continuously, on a sampling basis, or on an ad hoc basis. For analysis we may use all the data available, or just select part of them. How often should data be collected, and how much data should be used for analysis are major operational decisions each data center must face. The more data is collected and used for analysis, the more costly the function of capacity planning. On the other hand, using more data may lead to more accurate interpretation of the existing conditions and prediction of the future requirements, thereby resulting in a more cost-effective solution. Therefore, some trade-off between processing overhead and analysis accuracy is inevitable. Question 8 in the questionnaire was designed to assess system monitoring practices by the Fortune companies.

4.3 Survey Methodology

A pilot questionnaire was designed to collect empirical information related to the critical issues discussed above. The pilot questionnaires were sent out in May 1985 to a sample of 40 companies chosen based on systematic sampling from the 1985 Fortune 1000 companies. A total of 10 responses (or 25%) were received. These responses were carefully analyzed before launching the full-scale survey.

The results from the pilot survey indicated that a study based on larger samples was feasible. It was also discovered that a few important variables were excluded from the pilot questionnaire and that there were some ambiguities. The questionnaire was revised accordingly and the final version is shown in the Appendix. The pilot survey also indicated that no major capacity planning practice issues have been omitted from the questionnaire.

Based on the experience of the pilot study, it was decided to survey 930 companies from the Fortune population of companies. The 40 companies in the pilot survey were not included in the full-scale survey. Also excluded were 30 companies that (we know from previous research experiences) do not respond to questionnaires of this kind as a matter of company policy. The full-scale survey was launched by the end of June 1985. The cover letters, questionnaires, and self-stamped return-addressed envelopes were sent to the Vice-President of Data Processing or to the President if the name of the VP cannot be located. Follow-up letters and copies of the questionnaires were sent to those firms which had not responded by July 31, 1985.

By early October 1985, we received a total of 388 usable responses (or about 42% response rate). These responses were analyzed and the results are presented in the next section. As shown in Table 4.1, these respondents represent a large variety of industries. To determine if there was any non-response bias (i.e. non-respondents holding view sig-

TABLE 4.1

USABLE RESPONSE TO THE QUESTIONNAIRE SURVEY
ON COMPUTER CAPACITY PLANNING PRACTICES

Industry	No. of Companies Responded
1. Aerospace	9
2. Apparel	3
3. Beverages	3
4. Chemicals	18
5. Electronics, Appliances	18
6. Food	18
7. Glass, Concrete, Abrasive Gypsum	5
8. Industrial and Farm Equipment	7
9. Jewelry, Silverware	1
10. Measuring, Scientific, Photographic Equipment	5
11. Metal Manufacturing	8
12. Metal Products	6
13. Mining, Crude-Oil Production	3
14. Motor Vehicles and Equipment	9
15. Office Equipment (includes computers)	8
16. Paper, Fiber, and Wood Products	12
17. Petroleum Refining	16
18. Pharmaceuticals	7
19. Publishing, Printing	4
20. Rubber, Plastic Products	7
21. Shipbuilding, Railroad and Transportation Equipment	3
22. Soaps	3
23. Textile, Vinyl Flooring	3
Total Industrial Companies	176
24. Commercial Banks	46
25. Diversified Financial Companies	35
26. Life Insurance Companies	32
27. Retailing Companies	15
28. Diversified Service Companies	40
29. Transportation Service Companies	10
30. Utilities	34
Total Service Companies	212
TOTAL OF ALL COMPANIES RESPONDED	388

nificantly different from the respondents), a chi-square test of homogeneity was conducted by comparing the responses from early respondents with those from respondents to follow-up letters (late respondents).   Late respondents were assumed to hold views similar to those of non-respondents.   (This is a commonly used methodology to detect non-response bias in questionnaire surveys of this kind.   See, for example, Oppenheim [1966].) Our test provided no indication of any significant non-response bias in the responses to the questionnaire at 0.05 level of significance.

4.4   Overall Average Ratings

Table 4.2 shows the average ratings for each of the questions 2 to 8 in the questionnaire. The ratings for these are designed on a 1 to 4 scale, with 1 meaning "the method is frequently used" and 4 meaning "the method is rarely or never used".   Therefore, the closer the average rating is to 1, the more commonly the method is applied in practice.

An analysis of variance was performed on the mean ratings for each question to see if the means as a group within each question are significantly different from each other.   Table 4.3 shows that there are significant differences among the mean ratings for each question. Multiple comparisons were also performed. Table 4.4 shows the results of multiple comparisons using the Ryan-Einot-Gabriel-Welsch F test [SAS 1985, pp. 113-119].   (Other tests were also performed and the results were similar.) We observe that most of the mean ratings within each

TABLE 4.2

OVERALL RATINGS FOR QUESTIONS 2 TO 8
IN THE QUESTIONNAIRE SURVEY

Definition of ratings: 1 = frequently used   2 = sometimes used
                       3 = occasionally used   4 = rarely/never used

Questions in Questionnaire Relating to Computer Capacity Planning Practices	Distribution of Ratings in Percentage				Average Rating
	1	2	3	4	
2. Methods used to determine when CPU upgrade is required					
a) Predict CPU utilization	70	16	7	7	1.50
b) Predict performance eg. response time	58	20	10	12	1.77
c) Predict technological innovations	15	27	33	25	2.67
3. Methods used to determine when disk upgrade is required					
a) Predict disk storage requirements	78	12	6	4	1.36
b) Predict data access rate	17	23	23	37	2.80
c) Predict response time	27	32	21	20	2.33
d) Predict technological innovations	14	26	31	29	2.76
e) Acquire new disk along with new CPU	11	20	24	45	3.03
4. Methods used to predict response time					
a) Plot and extrapolate	36	33	12	19	2.14
b) Use simple queueing models	16	26	20	38	2.80
c) Use queueing network models	12	9	21	58	3.25
d) Use performance modeling packages	23	14	16	46	2.85
e) Use synthetic load benchmarking	8	11	20	61	3.34
5. Methods used to establish performance objectives					
a) Based on past performance experiences	57	27	10	6	1.65
b) Based on industry-wide practice	11	25	28	36	2.89
c) Based on negotiations with major user groups	36	30	19	15	2.13
d) Based on extensive analysis of the effect of response time on user productivity	17	20	27	36	2.84
6. Methods used for projecting computer workload					
a) Visual trending	54	25	10	11	1.77
b) Use time-series regression	23	14	21	42	2.82
c) Use structural models	25	35	20	20	2.35
d) Use sophisticated forecasting techniques	3	4	12	81	3.70
e) Survey users for their own projections	31	29	19	21	2.30
7. Measurement of workload					
a) Total CPU hours consumed	50	24	13	13	1.88
b) CPU hours consumed by workload class	55	24	9	12	1.77
c) Transaction/job counts	50	26	13	11	1.84
d) Total composite measure units (e.g. service units on IBM systems)	26	19	21	34	2.62
e) Composite measure units by workload class	24	19	19	38	2.72
f) Traffic rate in communication network	33	25	19	23	2.32
8. Data collection and analysis practice					
a) Collect continuously and analyze all data	38	14	22	26	2.35
b) Collect contin'ly and analyze sample data	27	24	23	26	2.48
c) Collect and use sample data	23	25	22	30	2.59
d) Collect only as required at irregular intervals	11	19	19	51	3.10

TABLE 4.3

ANALYSIS OF VARIANCES FOR OVERALL MEAN RATINGS

Question	Computed F Value	Degrees of Freedom	Significant at 0.05 level
2	149.74	2;1161	Yes
3	166.68	4;1935	Yes
4	67.30	4;1795	Yes
5	112.37	3;1308	Yes
6	191.30	4;1935	Yes
7	54.59	5;2322	Yes
8	31.75	3;1548	Yes

TABLE 4.4

MULTIPLE COMPARISONS USING THE RYAN-EINOT-GABRIEL-WELSCH F TEST

Question	Mean Ratings Arranged in Ascending Order		Grouping*
2	1.50	(2a)	1
	1.77	(2b)	2
	2.67	(2c)	3
3	1.36	(3a)	1
	2.33	(3c)	2
	2.76	(3d)	3
	2.80	(3b)	3
	3.03	(3e)	4
4	2.14	(4a)	1
	2.80	(4b)	2
	2.85	(4d)	2
	3.25	(4c)	3
	3.34	(4e)	3
5	1.65	(5a)	1
	2.13	(5c)	2
	2.84	(5d)	3
	2.89	(5b)	3
6	1.77	(6a)	1
	2.30	(6e)	2
	2.35	(6c)	2
	2.82	(6b)	3
	3.70	(6d)	4
7	1.77	(7b)	1
	1.84	(7c)	1
	1.88	(7a)	1
	2.32	(7f)	2
	2.62	(7d)	3
	2.72	(7e)	3
8	2.35	(8a)	1
	2.48	(8b)	1
	2.59	(8c)	1
	3.10	(8d)	2

* For each question, mean ratings of the same grouping are not
   significantly different from each other at 0.05 level of
   significance.

question are significantly different from each other. However, there are some exceptions. For example, the first three options for data collection and analysis (8a, 8b, 8c) are used with about equal frequency. The implication of these exceptions will be explained later.

Interpretations of the results on overall ratings are presented in the following subsections. They are grouped according to the five critical computer capacity planning issues discussed in Section 4.2.

4.4.1 Approaches Used for Computer System Analysis

Questions 2 and 3 deal with the approaches used to analyze the system behavior as the basis for CPU and disk upgrade decisions, and Question 4 deals with specifically the techniques for performance prediction.

The ratings in Table 4.2 for Qeustion 2 and the test results in Tables 4.3 and 4.4 show that significantly more computer installations are using CPU utilization than computer performance or technological innovations as the basis for CPU upgrade. This result is not too surprising. CPU utilization has traditionally been used as the index for measuring the adequacy of computer capacity. The underlying assumption of this approach is that when CPU utilization exceeds a certain percentage, say 75%, the interactive response time will increase sharply and performance may no longer be acceptable. Although this may not be the case, such rules of thumb are relied on extensively in the past and are still widely used today according to our results. CPU utilization can be calculated easily from data provided by most commercially available software or hardware monitors. Furthermore, the intuitive relationship between utilization and capacity can easily be understood by management.

From the results of Question 2b, 58% of our survey respondents checked performance prediction as a frequently used means in their organizations to determine when a CPU upgrade will be required. This percentage is quite high, although not as high as the 70% for the CPU utilization prediction. This phenomenon indicates that a majority of the installations have recognized the importance of computer performance to the organization and are explicitly using this variable in decision makings for capacity planning. This is true for the upgrade of CPU, the most critical resource in a computer system.

The upgrade of disk systems has not followed the same pattern, however. Only 27% of our respondents frequently use response time prediction as a basis to determine the timing for disk upgrades. Decisions for disk system upgrade are based mostly on storage capacity as indicated in Tables 4.2 to 4.4. The volume of data access and transfer is used much less frequently. This indicates that capacity planners are more concerned with the growth of data storage requirements than data access and transfer rates.

From the results of Questions 2 and 3 in Tables 4.2 to 4.4, it is apparent that computer capacity planning in practice is still largely based on a component approach. With this approach, each major component (e.g., CPU, disk) is monitored and an upgrade decision is made based on that component's utilization. For disk systems, our results show that the major concern is the storage utilization. In the case of CPU, performance prediction is also used in addition to the CPU utilization. The prediction is based mostly on plotting and extrapolating of performance data against workload as will be discussed below.

Although not rated as a major approach, significant technological innovation as a basis for equipment upgrade has received attention (75% of the respondents use it for CPU upgrade and 71% use it for disk upgrade at least occasionally). With the rapid changes in electronic technologies, the improvement in price/performance ratio sometimes affects the cost and benefits analysis so much that it may be advantageous to time equipment upgrades to match the introduction of new products. However, the result also shows that only 14% of the respondents perform technological forecast frequently. An explanation of this low rating is that, while technological advances may provide good opportunities for computer facility upgrade, most companies act prudently. That is, they often prefer to make decisions based on proven products rather than predicted introduction of new products.

The methods used to predict response time are dealt with in Question 4. The distribution and the average of ratings are calculated for responses which have answered 1 to 3 for either Part b of Question 2 or Part c of Question 3. That is, if a company predicts response time at least occasionally, whether it is for CPU or for disk upgrades, the methods they use for the prediction as represented by their answers for Question 4 are calculated and shown in Table 4.2. The results indicate that the intuitive trending method is used most often. All the other methods that involve modeling receive rather low ratings. Even the use of performance modeling packages is rated as "rarely or never used" by

46% of the respondents although almost one quarter respondents said they use modeling packages frequently. An explanation for this phenomenon is that a great deal of inertia still exists among practitioners in the application of system modeling. For many organizations, the upfront effort required to set up these models are still too great. Furthermore, under zero-based budget, allocation of funds for various activities including capacity planning activities is prioritized. It may be that the current priority levels for capacity planning in many organizations only justify simpler and less costly approaches. Hence the modeling methods cannot be used frequently in these organizations. For major configuration changes in large and complex installations, it is advisable to examine the potential benefits that can be gained from the more sophisticated methods before discarding them merely on budgetary reasons.

4.4.2 Computer Performance and User Productivity

Question 5 in the questionnaire and part of Questions 2 and 3 deal with this issue. The results of Question 5 show that 85% of the companies responded have established performance objectives for their computer services. The distribution and the average of the ratings for Question 5 as shown in Table 4.2 are computed for these 85% responses. Explicit involvement of users through discussion and negotiation with major user groups is rated as a "sometimes use" approach (average rating 2.13, and 36% companies do it frequently). However, extensive analysis of the effect of the average and the variation of response time on user productivity is not yet widely performed in setting response time objectives (average rating 2.84) despite the amount of attention given in the published literature on this issue.

The most frequently used basis for establishing performance objectives is the installation's past performance experiences (57% of the respondents indicate that they use it frequently). This phenomenon is not unexpected. The past performance experiences provide not only a reference for what is deliverable given the existing computing environment, but also some feel for an acceptable performance level for the given user community and business requirements. This largely judgmental approach coupled with user feedback through discussions and negotiations with major user groups in establishing performance objectives often result in harmonious relationship between the computer center and the users, although a more scientific approach based on extensive analysis of the effect of computer performance on user productivity can be fruitful. Industry-wide practice is not used very often possibly due to the unavailability of suitable industry-wide data in this aspect.

The question regarding the direct use of projected computer performance (e.g., response time) as a criterion in equipment upgrades can be answered by Part b of Question 2 and Part c of Question 3. The average ratings show that the use of performance as a criterion for CPU upgrade decisions has gained wide recognition, even though it is still not as popular as the use of CPU utilization (average rating 1.77 versus 1.50). The role of interactive response time in the decisions for disk upgrades is much smaller, however. Only 27% of our respondents said they predict response time frequently for disk upgrade decisions, compared to 58% for CPU upgrades. This may be due to the fact that most disks are used for

data storage. According to our results, the expansion or upgrade of
disks is largely based on disk storage utilization (78% used this
criterion frequently). These results reflect that storage utilization
is still capacity planners' predominant concern on storage disk
upgrades. Not enough attention has been given to the impact of the performance of storage disks on the overall system performance. When a
user command involves the access to a file or database stored on a disk,
the disk access time constitutes a major part of the system's response
time to the user's request. The system modeling approach discussed in
Chapter 3 allows the incorporation of disks into the evaluation of the
overall system performance.

4.4.3 Computer Workload Forecast

From the average ratings for Question 6 in Table 4.2 and the test
results in Tables 4.3 and 4.4, visual trending is used significantly
more often than other methods for projecting computer workload (average
rating 1.77, 54% use it frequently). This indicates that subjective
judgment still plays an important role in workload forecast. Judgmental
approach can sometimes produce good forecasts, especially when the data
processing environment is not very complex, the growth of computer usage
is stable, and the forecaster is experienced. User's own computer
workload projections was rated only second to visual trending reflecting
the extent of user involvement in computer capacity planning. Involving
users in workload prejection is a way of enhancing users' management and
control of their own computer utilization.

Structural forecasting model is an attempt to relate computer workload forecast with business forecast. These models have been suggested in the literature on workload forecasting (see, for example, Sarna [1979], Bronner [1980]). The implementation of these models has been made easier with commercial software packages such as LISREL [Joreskog and Sorbom, 1981]. The usage of these models is rated moderately high (average rating 2.35). One advantage of these models is that they relate computer workload with business measures, thus appeal to the management more easily. Rating for the time series regression approach are surprisingly low (2.82 compared to 1.77 for visual trending) despite the availability of statistical packages that can perform regression analysis. Sophisticated forecasting techniques such as Box-Jenkins models are hardly used at all (average ratng 3.70, and 81% of the respondents rarely or never use it). The methodology is complex and costly. One difficulty in using the Box-Jenkins models lies with the requirement of a large number of data points (e.g. 50 or more) for proper model identification. This requirement can pose problem in capacity planning since many installations may not have such long term measurement data that is applicable to the current capacity study.

4.4.4 Computer Workload Measures

The average ratings for Question 7 given in Table 4.2 show that CPU hours by workload class is one of the most commonly used definition of computer workload (average rating 1.77). This indicates that the division of workload into different classes has become a common practice,

and that practitioners have realized the different impacts that different workload classes have on the capacity requirements.   Total CPU
hours consumed is also rated quite highly.   This high rating of total
CPU hours as the definition of computer workload is consistent with the
high rating of using CPU utilization as the basis for CPU upgrade
decisions.   The use of traffic rate in communications network is checked
as a frequently used definitions of computer workload by almost one
third of the respondents, indicatng the importance of networking in the
computing environment.   Tables 4.2 to 4.4 show that composite measures
such as service units are not used very often (significantly less than
other measures), possibly due to the difficulty in identifying the bottleneck resource from these measures.

4.4.5 System Monitoring

     This issue is dealt with in Question 8 and the results in Tables
4.2 and 4.4 show that the average ratings for the first three practices
are very close.   These results indicate that these three practices are
used with about the same frequency: (i) collect continuously and analyze
all data collected, (ii) collect continuously but analyze only sampled
data, and (iii) sample in both data collection and analysis.   All of
these three practices treat system monitoring as an on-going activity.
The approach of collecting data at irregular intervals only as needs
arise is much less common (only 11% respondents said they frequently use
this approach).   This implies that most computer installations view that
computer capacity planning is an on-going process.   When the scale of

operations is sufficiently large, regular monitoring becomes necessary. The up-to-date information on the existing situation and forecasts allows the computer center to be responsive to user needs. Configuration changes can therefore be properly planned and carried out and major headaches minimized.

4.5 Implication of Results

The average ratings from the survey responses presented in this chapter provide an understanding of the overall tendency in the current use of the various approaches and methods in the practice of computer capacity planning. The more significant implications of these results include:

(1) Decisions for equipment upgrades in practice are still largely based on historical trend patterns for each component's utilization (e.g., 75% for CPU utilization). Performance prediction is also practiced often in relation to CPU upgrades, using mostly the trending method. Many of the analytic and simulation techniques for performance modeling and prediction are not widely used even though performance modeling packages seem to have gained momentum in large installations.

For some installations, the time and effort required to use the analytical and simulation techniques may be prohibitive. In this case, the component approach based on predefined utilization thresholds will serve useful purposes. For other installations, they may well afford to use these modeling techniques to their advantage, but are hesitant to invest much resources upfront for starting and ongoing expenses for continuing to use these techniques. This is evidenced by comments from some respondents who expressed their doubt on the usefulness of these techniques when the workload projections are often only crude estimates. The overall rating averages indicate the percentage of Fortune companies that are using the modeling approach. The next chapter will present the environment in which modeling is likely being applied. These results should provide encouragement for those installations who are considering the use of system modeling but are hesitant to do so at this time. To widen the application even further, future research in this area should include the effect of workload uncertainty on the results of these scientific techniques.

(2) Most computer installations have established performance objectives in their operations. Past performance experience is often used as the basis for setting these objectives. Interactive response time is an important performance index in most computer systems and is generally perceived to have important effect on user productivity. In establishing the response time objectives, however, not many organizations conduct extensive analysis of the effect of computer response time on user productivity despite what is being proposed in the literature. Judgmental approach based on past experiences and discussions with users is more prevalent in practice. What is needed for most organizations is a convenient and convincing measure of this effect and the cost of productivity loss due to inadequate response time.

(3) Visual trending from historical data plus anticipated new work

is still the most popular approach in workload forecasting. Among the scientific approaches, structural models seem to be more readily accepted than others. The strongest appeal of the structural models approach is its capability to include user-oriented measures in the forecasting, thus allowing meaningful user input to this vital aspect of capacity planning. Further development on this approach by researchers and managers can be fruitful.

(4) Workload continues to mean different things to different people. There is no consensus on what is the best definition. Suitably selected measures of computer workload are important not only for capacity planners to properly plan computer capacity to meet future needs, but also for auditors and other quality assurance personnel in their measurement and evaluation of the performance of their computer facilities.

A composite workload measure allows the incorporation of work performed by the major components in the system. It can be used as a billing unit, and can simplify workload projections from user departments. The computer center does require supplementary data for the purpose of performance evaluation and capacity planning. This type of measures is not yet being commonly used. To widen its acceptance, more user friendly software packages which integrate the facilities for related functions such as billing, workload reporting by user and by application, utilization and performance monitoring and reporting based on the composite measures will be necessary. Moreover, appropriate and convenient to use algorithms must be developed to allow proper conversion and smooth transition from the composite measure of the current configuration to the measure of the next configuration.

(5) Resources expended on system monitoring is generally viewed as overhead. It is therefore desirable to minimize the cost of system monitoring while maintaining the quality of the planning process. Sampling appears to be a compromise between the approach of continuous monitoring and the ad hoc approach that collects data only as required. Sampling is actually being used in many computer measurement facilities to obtain data such as disk storage usage. However, sampling techniques are often used without thorough understanding of the implications. This subject deserves much more attention by researchers in the area of performance evaluation and capacity planning.

(6) While the methodology used and the issues emphasized are quite different between our survey and those of Kelly [1983] and Morino Associates [1983], some of our results are found to be consistent with theirs. For example, Kelly found that there was a lack of standaridized workload measures and that the primary measure of capacity was utilization. Our survey results confirm these findings and provided a more indepth analysis of the issue. Both our study and the report by Morino Associates found that a high percentage of installations has established user-oriented performance objectives.

4.6 Summary

The importance of computer capacity planning is widely recognized. Many existing publications discuss the principles and techniques of computer capacity planning. It was felt that more work needs to be done to assess the extent that these principles and techniques have been applied in practice. What is happening in practice in this vital aspect of computer management is of interest to practitioners, researchers, auditors and other concerned parties.

This chapter presented a study designed to investigate the practice of computer capacity planning. A questionnaire survey was used to collect data directly from the Fortune companies. The design of the questionnaire, the survey methodology, the overall average rating of the responses, the associated statistical tests, and the implications of these overall rating results have been discussed in this chapter. In the next chapter we will present the environmental characteristics of the respondent companies, and assess the effect of these environmental characteristics on computer capacity planning practices.

                        Appendix -- The Questionnaire

          COMPUTER CAPACITY PLANNING PRACTICE QUESTIONNAIRE

General Instructions:

(i)   For purpose of this questionnaire, computer capacity planning is
       defined as the function to monitor and project computer workload
       and to manage and plan for changes or expansions of computer con-
       figurations to meet projected future damands.

(ii)   In questions 2 to 8, the ratings are defined as follows:
       1 = frequently use   2 = sometimes use
       3 = occasionally use   4 = rarely/never use

       Circle your answers in these questions. For example, if question
       2 method a is frequently used by your data center, circle 1, and
       if method b is only occasionally used, circle 3, etc.

Question 1:
       Check the principal computer facility currently installed in your
data center.

       a) Mainframe   IBM30XX [ ]   IBM370 [ ]   CDC [ ]   Honeywell [ ]
                       Burroughs [ ]   Univac [ ]
                       Others (specify_____) [ ]
       b) Mini: VAX [ ]   Prime [ ]   Data General [ ]   Wang [ ]
                       Others (specify_____) [ ]

Question 2:
       Rate the following methods in terms of their use for your data
center's principal computer facility for determining when an upgrade of
the CPU capacity is required. (For a and b below, prediction is to be
on growth of existing workload and anticipated new systems/
applications.)
                                                                 Ratings
       a) Predict when CPU utilization will reach a
          threshold. (Specify threshold used:_____)   1 2 3 4
       b) Predict when performance (e.g., response time,
          turnaround time) will reach a threshold, and CPU
          is determined to be the bottleneck. (Specify
          thresholds used:_____)   1 2 3 4
       c) Predict when significant technological innovations
          will occur.   1 2 3 4
       d) Other (specify_____)   1 2 3 4

Appendix (cont'd)

Question 3:
    Rate the following methods in terms of their use for your data
center's principal computer facility for determining when an <u>upgrade of
the disk configuration</u> is required. (For a, b, and c below, prediction
is to be based on growth trends and anticipated new systems/
applications.)

Ratings

a) Predict when disk storage requirements will exceed
   existing capacity.   1 2 3 4
b) Predict when disk accesses per second (or data
   transfer per second) will reach a threshold.
   (Specify threshold used:_____)   1 2 3 4
c) Predict when interactivve response time will reach
   a threshold, and disk is determined to be the
   bottleneck. (Specify threshold used:_____)   1 2 3 4
d) Predict when significant technological innovations
   will occur.   1 2 3 4
e) Acquire new disk models along with new CPU.   1 2 3 4
f) Other (Specify_____)   1 2 3 4

Question 4:
    Rate the following methods in terms of their use for your data
center's principal computer facility for <u>Predicting response time</u> of interactive transactions.

Ratings

a) Identify a trend from plots of response time
   versus workload, and extrapolate the trend to the
   projected workload level.   1 2 3 4
b) Use simple queueing models to estimate queueing time
   in each of the major components (e.g., communications
   network, CPU, I/O channel, disk, etc.).   1 2 3 4
c) Use sophisticated queueing network models where
   multiple resources in the computer system can be
   represented in a network of queues, and overall
   performance for each workload class is obtained.   1 2 3 4
d) Use performace modeling packages (e.g., BEST/1,
   MAP, etc.).   1 2 3 4
e) Use synthetic load benchmarking where workload is
   simulated based on a script of the benchmark load,
   and response time is measured under various loading
   factors applied in the simulation.   1 2 3 4
f) Other (Specify_____)   1 2 3 4

Question 5:
    Does your center have performace objectives for the major workload
types (e.g., average response time 2 seconds, 95th percentile within 5
second, etc.)?   YES [ ]   NO [ ]

Appendix (cont'd)

If yes, rate the following methods in terms of their use in <u>es-tablishing these performance objectives</u> for your data center's principal computer facility:

<u>Ratings</u>

a) Based on past performance experience. 1 2 3 4
b) Based on industry-wide practice. 1 2 3 4
c) Based on discussion/negotiations with major user groups. 1 2 3 4
d) Based on extensive analysis of the effect of response time on user productivity. 1 2 3 4
e) Other (Specify_____) 1 2 3 4

Question 6:
Rate the following methods in terms of their use for your data center's principal computer facility for <u>projecting computer workload</u>.

<u>Ratings</u>

a) Visual trending from historical workload data plus anticipated new work. 1 2 3 4
b) Scientific trending using regression techniques plus anticipated new work. 1 2 3 4
c) Identify relationship between computer workload and key factors (e.g., sales volume, computer budget, number of terminals in the network, etc.). Then use this relationship to project workload from predicted values of these key factors. 1 2 3 4
d) Use sophisticated forecasting techniques (e.g., ARIMA or Box-Jenkins Models, Delphi Analyses, etc.) 1 2 3 4
e) Survey major user groups for their own projections. 1 2 3 4
f) Other (Specify_____) 1 2 3 4

Question 7:
Rate the following quantities in terms of their use as <u>definition of computer workload</u> for the purpose of capacity planning for your data center's principal computer facility.

<u>Ratings</u>

a) Total number of CPU hours consumed. 1 2 3 4
b) Number of CPU hours consumed for each workload class (interactive, batch, database, etc.) 1 2 3 4
c) Number of transactions executed for interactive workload, and number of jobs executed for batch. 1 2 3 4
d) Total number of service units (a weighted sum of the utilization of critical resources including CPU, memory, and I/O) consumed. 1 2 3 4
e) Number of service units consumed for each workload class. 1 2 3 4
f) Number of transactions transmitted per second in the communication network. 1 2 3 4
g) Other (Specify_____) 1 2 3 4

Appendix (cont'd)

Question 8:
    Rate the following schemes in terms of their use in <u>workload and performance data collection and analysis</u> for your data center's principal computer facility.

Ratings

a) Collect detailed data continuously and use all
   available data in analysis.   1 2 3 4
b) Collect detailed data continuously but use only
   sampled data in analysis.   1 2 3 4
c) Collect data periodically at selected days and
   hours (i.e.,sampling) and use these sampled data
   in analysis.   1 2 3 4
d) Collect data for analysis as required at
   irregular intervals.   1 2 3 4
e) Other (Specify_____)   1 2 3 4

Question 9:
    Please indicate the <u>significance of each class of workload</u> as a percentage of the total workload in your data center's principal computer facility.

	0-25%	26-50%	51-75%	76-100%
a) Interactive	[ ]	[ ]	[ ]	[ ]
b) Batch	[ ]	[ ]	[ ]	[ ]
c) Database	[ ]	[ ]	[ ]	[ ]
d) Other (Specify____)	[ ]	[ ]	[ ]	[ ]

Question 10:
    Please indicate the number of staff responsible for the computer capacity planning functions in your data center_____.

Question 11:
    Please indicate the <u>computer utilization for capacity planning</u> as a percentage of the total workload in your data center's principal computer facility.
    a) 5% or below [ ]   b) 6 to 15% [ ]
    c) 16 to 25%   [ ]   d) Over 25% [ ]

Question 12:
    The budget for your data center's <u>computer operations</u> (include hardware purchase/rental, software purchase/license, and manpower) in 1985 is (check one):
    a) $10 million or below [ ]   b) $11 to $30 million [ ]
    c) $31 to $50 million   [ ]   d) Over $50 million   [ ]

Question 13:
    Does your data center charge back to users for their use of the principal computer facility?
    No Charge [ ]   Partly Charge [ ]   Fully Charge [ ]

Appendix (cont'd)

Please feel free to provide any further comments on computer capacity planning practices in your firm. Please also indicate if you would like to receive a copy of the summary report. Thank you for your kind assistance.

CHAPTER 5

COMPUTER CAPACITY PLANNING PRACTICES

5.1 Introduction

A wide range of tools and techniques exist for the various aspects
of computer capacity planning, as discussed in Chapters 2 and 3.
Workload forecasting, for example, may be based on visual trending,
time-series regression, structural models, Box-Jenkins models, and so
on. Response time may also be predicted using the trend and
extrapolation, queueing network modeling, synthetic load benchmarking,
and so on. Clearly not all methods are suitable for every installation.
A capacity planner should select a method that suits his or her
installation's environment. To this end, the experiences of other organizations with similar environment should provide useful guidelines as
to what may be appropriate. An important objective of our survey study
is to solicit relevant information from the business data processing installations to allow characterizations of companies based on a number of
environmental factors. This chapter presents the results of such a
characterization and analyzes how practices may be different under dif-

ferent environment.

In the next section we first present a profile of the respondents to our survey study in terms of their computing and business environments. The environmental factors and the rationale behind their selection for analysis will be discussed in Section 5.3. Sections 5.4 and 5.5 will analyze how these factors affect capacity planning practices based on our survey results, and Section 5.6 will discuss the implication of these results. A brief summary of the chapter is given in Section 5.7 .

5.2 Computing and Business Environments of Respondents

To allow characterizations of companies based on a number of environmental factors, we have included several questions in the questionnaire to help identify the computing and business environments of the respondents to the survey study. These questions enquire about:

. Principal computer facility

. Percentage of interactive usage

. Percentage of database usage

. Percentage of computer utilization for computer capacity planning

. Amount of computer operation budget

. Extent of charging for computer services

In addition, companies are also characterized based on their type of industry as stated in the Fortune Directories [Fortune 1985]. Three different groups are of particular interest because of the differences in the nature of their operations: Industrial vs. Service Companies, Financial vs. Non-Financial Companies, and High Tech vs. Non-High Tech Companies. (The reasons for selecting these factors for characterizations will be discussed in the next section.)

The breakdown among respondents based on each characterization is presented in Table 5.1. Some highlights of these results are noted below.

(1) A great majority (84%) of the companies responded use IBM or IBM compatible mainframes as their principal computer facilities. It should be noted that some of these companies also use computer systems from other vendors, but not as their principal facilities.

(2) Interactive mode is the most dominating mode of computer usage. About one third of the respondents' interactive usage is over 50% of the total computer workload, whereas only 19% of the respondents said their batch usage is over 50% of the total, and 8% of the respondents said their database usage is over 50% of the total.

(3) The use of computers for the function of capacity planning is not especially high. Eighty-seven percent of the respondents said their utilization for this function is less than 5% of the total computer utilization.

(4) The budget for computer data processing is substantial. More than one third (37%) of the respondents have over $10 million budgeted

TABLE 5.1

BREAKDOWN AMONG RESPONDENTS BASED ON
DIFFERENT ENVIRONMENTAL CHARACTERISTICS

Environmental variables	Breakdown among respondents	
	Number	Percentage
1. Computer facility:		
IBM (or compatible) mainframe	324	84
Non-IBM mainframe	40	10
Mini	24	6
2. Interactive usage:		
0-25% of total	86	22
26-50% of total	177	46
51-75% of total	95	24
76-100% of total	30	8
3. Data Base usage:		
0-25% of total	255	66
26-50% of total	101	26
51-75% of total	26	7
76-100% of total	6	1
4. Computer utilization for Capacity Planning:		
Low ($\leq$ 5% of total)	336	87
High (> 5% of total)	41	11
No answer	11	2
5. Computer Budget:		
Low ($\leq$ $10 million)	238	61
High (> $10 Million)	144	37
No answer	6	2
6. Charging:		
No charge	95	24
Partly Charge	102	26
Fully charge	188	49
No answer	3	1
7. Industry: Industrial	176	45
Service	212	55
8. Industry: Financial	113	29
Non-Financial	275	71
9. Industry: High Tech	35	9
Non-High Tech	353	91

in 1985.

(5) Direct charging for computer services is a common practice. Only 24% of the responding companies do not charge while almost half of the respondents fully charge for these services.

5.3 Potential Environmental Factors

Companies with different environmental characteristics may have different computer capacity planning practices. In this section nine factors are analyzed for their potentially significant effects on these practices.

(1) Computer Facilities

The majority of users in the business community uses IBM or IBM compatible mainframe systems. Among the respondents of our question- naire survey, 84% use them. Due to the huge market available, develop- ments of software packages are often targeted for IBM systems first. Performance measurement and capacity analysis software is no exception. It is expected that, with the availability of more such software, IBM installations will be more likely to conduct more detailed and possibly more sophisticated quantitative analysis for capacity planning. Furthermore, due to the big difference in price, the amount of effort involved in upgrading a minicomputer system is expected to be much less than that in a mainframe system. Hence, more crude approaches are ex- pected for minicomputer installations. Consequently, computer facility grouped as IBM mainframe, non-IBM mainframe, and minicomputer has been chosen as a factor to account for possible differences in computer capacity planning practices.

(2) Extent of Interactive Usage

With the development of computer terminals and communications network, computers have become more visible and directly available to users, and the mode of computer usage is increasingly more interactive. As a result, computer system performance in terms of response time becomes a major concern in computer operation management. It is therefore quite possible that the higher the percentage of interactive usage in an installation, the more emphasis will be placed on the measurement and prediction of the user-oriented performance indexes such as response time and turnaround time. Thus the percentage of interactive usage (and vice versa, batch usage) was selected as a factor for the comparison of capacity planning practices.

(3) Extent of Database Usage

The development of data base also has the effect of bringing computers closer to the user. Furthermore, with database systems, the on-line storage becomes a major concern. Therefore, the percentage of database usage was expected to have an impact on the capacity planning practices.

(4) Computer Utilization for Computer Capacity Planning

To monitor and predict system performance, and to track and forecast computer workload require computer resources. The more sophisticated the methods used, the more computer resources are expected to be utilized. It was, therefore, decided to select computer utilization for the capacity planning function as a factor in the analysis. Due to the diversity of computer systems involved, the computer utilization for capacity planning as a percentage of the total computer workload was used as a basis for comparison of computer capacity planning practices.

(5)   Computer Budget

The bigger the computer budget is for an installation, the more detailed planning is expected. Furthermore, with a large installation, more staff will be involved in the capacity planning function. It is then more likely to include staff with expertise in many aspects of planning. Consequently, more sophisticated techniques are expected to be applied.

(6)   Extent of Direct Charging

Many computer installations charge out for their computer services but others still do not charge at all. And yet some companies charge for some services but not for others. When services are charged out, it is expected that users will be more careful about the cost of the services they receive. As a result, performance and services become a more visible set of objectives for the computer operations management. The greater the extent of direct charging of computer services, the more emphasis is expected for ensuring adequate performance. The extent of direct charging was, therefore, selected as a factor for analyses.

(7)   Industrial versus Service Companies

The Fortune 1000 companies are grouped as Industrial 500 and Service 500 due to the difference in the types of business involved. The use of computers can be quite different between the two groups. As a result, the emphasis in the various aspects of computer capacity planning between the two groups of companies may be different. It is felt that, however, the diverse lines of business within each group may average out the effect of each other. To find out if this is indeed the case, the grouping of Industrial versus Service according to the Fortune listing was used as a factor for comparing capacity planning practices.

(8)   Financial versus Non-Financial Companies

Financial institutions such as banks and insurance companies are well known for their need for real time processing and their dependence on the nation-wide computer networks. These characteristics may impose very different requirements on an installation's implementation of capacity planning. We intend to investigate this factor by comparing the practices of financial versus non-financial respondents.

(9)   High Tech versus Non-High Tech Companies

The High Tech industry is expected to be a leader in their use of computers which should logically include the use of advanced techniques for computer capacity planning. For example, IBM frequently developed analysis tools for its internal users which were often enhanced and turned into commercial packages. It was therefore decided to compare the practices based on the High Tech versus Non-High Tech industry groupings.

5.4 Important Environmental Factors

For each of the nine environmental factors listed in Table 5.1,
statistical tests of significance using analysis of variance (AOV) based
on the conventional 95% level of significance were performed. Four of
the nine factors were found to be particularly important in that they
significantly affect all aspects of computer capacity planning practices
as represented by Questions 2 to 8 in the questionnaire. These four important environmental factors are: computer facility, computer budget,
extent of direct charging, and the financial vs. non-financial industry
characteristics. The mean ratings by group under the classification of
each of these four factors, and the statistical test results on the differences among these mean ratings are shown in Tables 5.2 and 5.3,
respectively. Table 5.4 summarizes the specific effects these factors
have on the various aspects of computer capacity planning based on the
test statistics. The effects presented in Table 5.4 are grouped according to the five critical computer capacity planning issues discussed in
Chapter 4. Analyses on the observed effects due to each of the four important environmental factors are provided in the subsections below.

Our analyses will concentrate on those effects that are statistically significant as shown in Table 5.3.

5.4.1 Computer Facility

Most of the effects that this IBM/Non-IBM/Mini classification has
on the various aspects of capacity planning practices can be explained

TABLE 5.2

MEAN RATINGS BY GROUP
BASED ON THE FOUR MOST SIGNIFICANT ENVIRONMENTAL FACTORS

Definition of ratings: 1 = frequently used   2=sometimes used
                        3 = occasionally used   4=rarely/never used

Questions in Questionnaire Relating to Capacity Planning Practices

2. Methods used to determine when CPU upgrade is required
   a) Predict CPU utilization
   b) Predict performance eg. response time
   c) Predict technological innovations

3. Methods used to determine when disk upgrade is required
   a) Predict disk storage requirements
   b) Predict data access rate
   c) Predict response time
   d) Predict technological innovations
   e) Acquire new disk along with new CPU

4. Methods used to predict response time
   a) Plot and extrapolate
   b) Use simple queuing models
   c) Use queuing network models
   d) Use performance modeling packages
   e) Use synthetic load benchmarking

5. Methods used to establish performance objectives
   a) Based on past performance experiences
   b) Based on industry-wide practice
   c) Based on negotiations with major user groups
   d) Based on extensive analysis of the effect of response time
      on user productivity

6. Methods used for projecting computer workload
   a) Visual trending plus expected new work
   b) Use time-series regression plus expected new work
   c) Use structural models
   d) Use sophisticated forecasting techniques
   e) Survey users for their own projections

7. Measurement of workload
   a) Total CPU hours consumed
   b) CPU hours consumed by workload class
   c) Transaction/job counts
   d) Total composite measure units eg. IBM service units
   e) Composite measure units by workload class
   f) Traffic rate in communication network

8. Data collection and analysis practice
   a) Collect continuously and analyze all data
   b) Collect continuously and analyze sample data
   c) Collect and use sample data
   d) Collect data on an ad hoc basis

TABLE 5.2 (Cont'd)

Mean Ratings by Group

	IBM	Computer Facility Non-IBM	Mini	Computer Budget <$10m*	>$10m*	Extent of Direct Charging NC**	PC**	FC**	Industry Characteristics F**	NF**
2.										
a	1.44	1.68	2.13	1.66	1.26	1.88	1.38	1.38	1.46	1.52
b	1.74	1.85	2.00	1.83	1.65	2.09	1.75	1.61	1.63	1.82
c	2.66	2.75	2.71	2.86	2.38	2.97	2.56	2.56	2.55	2.72
3.										
a	1.32	1.33	1.88	1.42	1.26	1.61	1.30	1.26	1.30	1.38
b	2.84	2.40	3.00	2.92	2.61	2.97	2.83	2.70	2.60	2.89
c	2.33	2.23	2.50	2.40	2.21	2.45	2.33	2.28	2.25	2.37
d	2.74	2.90	2.75	2.90	2.53	3.03	2.66	2.67	2.57	2.84
e	3.09	2.58	2.92	3.05	2.97	2.13	2.89	3.03	2.98	3.04
4.										
a	2.10	2.17	2.74	2.18	2.04	2.49	2.05	2.03	1.94	2.22
b	2.78	2.80	2.95	2.95	2.54	3.10	2.77	2.66	2.52	2.91
c	3.25	3.17	3.37	3.47	2.90	3.49	3.28	3.11	2.98	3.36
d	2.61	3.06	3.21	3.12	2.46	3.00	3.01	2.72	2.50	3.00
e	3.37	3.06	3.42	3.42	3.23	3.54	3.37	3.24	3.33	3.34
5.										
a	1.63	1.68	1.86	1.64	1.67	1.76	1.58	1.63	1.63	1.65
b	2.91	2.62	3.00	2.94	2.81	2.93	2.85	2.88	2.91	2.88
c	2.14	2.15	1.71	2.25	1.97	2.17	2.17	2.07	1.95	2.20
d	2.88	2.50	2.71	2.98	2.71	2.99	2.72	2.67	2.75	2.88
6.										
a	1.77	1.63	1.96	1.69	1.83	2.03	1.59	1.72	1.84	1.74
b	2.72	3.18	3.50	3.13	2.32	3.27	2.83	2.57	2.73	2.86
c	2.37	2.05	2.67	2.45	2.19	2.46	2.28	2.35	2.14	2.44
d	3.69	3.75	3.75	3.82	3.51	3.78	3.77	3.62	3.65	3.72
e	2.30	2.33	2.17	2.50	1.97	2.44	2.45	2.13	2.25	2.32
7.										
a	1.86	1.88	2.17	1.89	1.90	1.93	2.02	1.77	2.04	1.81
b	1.67	2.10	2.54	1.90	1.58	1.98	1.99	1.55	1.73	1.79
c	1.73	2.28	2.58	1.95	1.69	2.15	1.82	1.71	1.74	1.88
d	2.59	2.65	2.96	2.74	2.40	2.92	2.70	2.41	2.54	2.65
e	2.65	3.00	3.13	2.83	2.53	3.07	2.76	2.51	2.59	2.77
f	2.29	2.25	2.75	2.45	2.12	2.51	2.35	2.22	1.95	2.47
8.										
a	2.27	2.63	2.96	2.54	2.07	2.66	2.52	2.11	2.64	2.23
b	2.47	2.45	2.67	2.60	2.30	2.65	2.49	2.38	2.28	2.56
c	2.62	2.05	3.00	2.56	2.64	2.54	2.50	2.66	2.39	2.67
d	3.16	2.90	2.67	3.03	3.24	3.00	2.95	3.23	3.07	3.12

* "m" denotes a million dollars.
** NC = No Charge, PC = Partly Charge, FC = Fully Charge,
    F = Financial, NF = Non-Financial

TABLE 5.3

F TEST (ONE-WAY ANALYSIS OF VARIANCE) FOR THE DIFFERENCE IN
MEAN RATINGS

Questions in Questionnaire Relating to Capacity Planning Practices

---

2. Methods used to determine when CPU upgrade is required
   a) Predict CPU utilization
   b) Predict performance eg. response time
   c) Predict technological innovations

3. Methods used to determine when disk upgrade is required
   a) Predict disk storage requirements
   b) Predict data access rate
   c) Predict response time
   d) Predict technological innovations
   e) Acquire new disk along with new CPU

4. Methods used to predict response time
   a) Plot and extrapolate
   b) Use simple queuing models
   c) Use queuing network models
   d) Use performance modeling packages
   e) Use synthetic load benchmarking

5. Methods used to establish performance objectives
   a) Based on past performance experiences
   b) Based on industry-wide practice
   c) Based on negotiations with major user groups
   d) Based on extensive analysis of the effect of response time
      on user productivity

6. Methods used for projecting computer workload
   a) Visual trending plus expected new work
   b) Use time-series regression plus expected new work
   c) Use structural models
   d) Use sophisticated forecasting techniques
   e) Survey users for their own projections

7. Measurement of workload
   a) Total CPU hours consumed
   b) CPU hours consumed by workload class
   c) Transaction/job counts
   d) Total composite measure units eg. IBM service units
   e) Composite measure units by workload class
   f) Traffic rate in communication network

8. Data collection and analysis practice
   a) Collect continuously and analyze all data
   b) Collect continuously and analyze sample data
   c) Collect and use sample data
   d) Collect data on an ad hoc basis

TABLE 5.3 (Cont'd)

F Test Results

	Computer Facility p-value*	Sig*	Computer Budget p-value*	Sig*	Extent of Direct Charging p-value*	Sig*	Financial vs. Non-Financial p-value*	Sig*
2.								
a	0.0005**	Yes	0.0001	Yes	0.0001	Yes	0.5471	No
b	0.4328	No	0.1016	No	0.0010	Yes	0.0446	Yes
c	0.8464	No	0.0001	Yes	0.0022	Yes	0.1296	No
3.								
a	0.0024	Yes	0.0590	No	0.0008	Yes	0.3627	No
b	0.0420	Yes	0.0076	Yes	0.1579	No	0.0217	Yes
c	0.6188	No	0.0894	No	0.4382	No	0.3253	No
d	0.6490	No	0.0006	Yes	0.0098	Yes	0.0177	Yes
e	0.0112	Yes	0.4801	No	0.2821	No	0.5997	No
4.								
a	0.0512	No	0.2449	No	0.0050	Yes	0.0285	Yes
b	0.8272	No	0.0006	Yes	0.0145	Yes	0.0031	Yes
c	0.8030	No	0.0001	Yes	0.0226	Yes	0.0017	Yes
d	0.0468	Yes	0.0001	Yes	0.0423	Yes	0.0004	Yes
e	0.1848	No	0.0766	No	0.0590	No	0.9441	No
5.								
a	0.6403	No	0.8099	No	0.4235	No	0.7966	No
b	0.2509	No	0.2428	No	0.8917	No	0.7688	No
c	0.0370	Yes	0.0212	Yes	0.6985	No	0.0463	Yes
d	0.1451	No	0.0430	Yes	0.0492	Yes	0.3172	No
6.								
a	0.4360	No	0.1835	No	0.0059	Yes	0.3633	No
b	0.0012	Yes	0.0001	Yes	0.0001	Yes	0.3237	No
c	0.0658	No	0.0176	Yes	0.4857	No	0.0116	Yes
d	0.8327	No	0.0001	Yes	0.0870	No	0.3263	No
e	0.8374	No	0.0001	Yes	0.0194	Yes	0.5849	No
7.								
a	0.3908	No	0.9345	No	0.1437	No	0.0629	No
b	0.0001	Yes	0.0037	Yes	0.0002	Yes	0.6586	No
c	0.0001	Yes	0.0168	Yes	0.0027	Yes	0.2319	No
d	0.3370	No	0.0078	Yes	0.0025	Yes	0.4239	No
e	0.0522	No	0.0159	Yes	0.0007	Yes	0.1844	No
f	0.1604	No	0.0084	Yes	0.1457	No	0.0001	Yes
8.								
a	0.0102	Yes	0.0003	Yes	0.0004	Yes	0.0033	Yes
b	0.7157	No	0.0127	Yes	0.1641	No	0.0291	Yes
c	0.0021	Yes	0.5321	No	0.4686	No	0.0290	Yes
d	0.0401	Yes	0.0661	No	0.0549	No	0.7026	No

*   p-value = probability value;
    Sig = Statistically Significant at 0.05 level
** For example, this test shows that the difference among the mean
    ratings 1.44, 1.68 and 2.13 in Table 5.2 is significant.

TABLE 5.4

SPECIFIC EFFECTS OF THE FOUR MOST SIGNIFICANT ENVIRONMENTAL FACTORS
ON THE FIVE CRITICAL CAPACITY PLANNING ISSUES

Issue \ Factor	(1) Computer Facility IBM / Non-IBM / Mini
1) Approaches Used For Computer System Analysis	1. Compared with mini computer users, both mainframe groups (IBM and Non-IBM) place greater reliance on the formal prediction of future scenarios (utilization for CPU, storage requirements and data access rate for disk) in making equipment upgrade decisions. 2. The IBM group uses performance modeling packages for response time prediction more often than others.
2) Computer Performance and User Productivity	1. The minicomputer group sets performance objectives based on negotiations and discussions with users more often than the mainframe groups.
3) Computer Workload Forecast	1. Both mainframe groups perform time-series regression more often than the mini group, and the IBM group does it more often than the non-IBM.
4) Computer Workload Measures	1. Both mainframe groups measure the workload by class and use transaction/job counts more often than the mini group and the IBM group does it more often than the non-IBM.
5) System Monitoring	1. The IBM group tends to collect continuously and analyze all data; the non-IBM mainframe group tends to collect and analyze sampled data; and the mini group often collects and analyzes data on an ad hoc basis.

TABLE 5.4 (Cont'd)

SPECIFIC EFFECTS OF THE FOUR MOST SIGNIFICANT ENVIRONMENTAL FACTORS
ON THE FIVE CRITICAL CAPACITY PLANNING ISSUES

Factor / Issue	(2) Computer Budget Large (> $10 million)/ Small (≤ $10 million)
1) Approaches Used For Computer System Analysis	1. Compared with the small budget group, the large budget group places greater reliance on the formal prediction of future scenarios (utilization for CPU, data access rate for disk) in making equipment upgrade decisions. 2. Prediction of technological innovations is practiced more often by the large budget group. 3. The large budget group rated the use of analytical techniques and performance modeling packages for predicting response time much higher than the small budget group.
2) Computer Performance and User Productivity	1. The large budget group performs extensive analysis on the effects of response time on user productivity in setting response time objectives, more often than the small budget group.
3) Computer Workload Forecast	1. The large budget group applies the advanced quantitative techniques for workload forecast more often than the small budget group.
4) Computer Workload Measures	1. Workload measures other than the total CPU hours consumed are monitored more often by the large budget group.
5) System Monitoring	1. The large budget group tends to collect more detailed data and use more data for analysis.

TABLE 5.4 (Cont'd)

SPECIFIC EFFECTS OF THE FOUR MOST SIGNIFICANT ENVIRONMENTAL FACTORS
ON THE FIVE CRITICAL CAPACITY PLANNING ISSUES

Factor Issue	(3) Extent of Direct Charging Fully Charge/Partly Charge/No Charge
1) Approaches Used For Computer System Analysis	1. The charging groups rely more on formal prediction of future scenarios (utilization for CPU, storage requirements for disk) for their equipment upgrade decisions. 2. Prediction of technological innovations is practiced more often by the charging groups. 3. The more an installation charges, the more often it uses the various tools for response time predictions.
2) Computer Performance and User Productivity	1. The fully charge group tends to establish performance objectives based on extensive analysis of the effects of response time on user productivity more often than others. 2. The more an installation charges, the more often it conducts performance predictions for its CPU upgrade decisions.
3) Computer Workload Forecast	1. The charging groups project workload more often than the non-charging group using trending, regression, and user surveys.
4) Computer Workload Measures	1. Workload measures other than the total CPU hours consumed and network traffic are monitored significantly more often by the charging groups.
5) System Monitoring	1. The fully charge group tends to collect continuously and use all data for analysis.

TABLE 5.4 (Cont'd)

SPECIFIC EFFECTS OF THE FOUR MOST SIGNIFICANT ENVIRONMENTAL FACTORS
ON THE FIVE CRITICAL CAPACITY PLANNING ISSUES

Issue \ Factor	(4) Industry Characteristics Financial/Non-Financial
1) Approaches Used For Computer System Analysis	1. Prediction of technological innovations is practiced more often by the financial group for their disk upgrade decisions. 2. The financial group uses the various tools for response time predictions more often than the non-financial group.
2) Computer Performance and User Productivity	1. The financial group sets performance objectives based on negotiations with users more often than the other group. 2. The financial group conducts performance predictions in their CPU upgrade decisions more often than the other group.
3) Computer Workload Forecast	1. The financial group uses structural models for workload forecast more often than the non-financial group.
4) Computer Workload Measures	1. Network traffic is used more often by the financial group as their workload measure.
5) System Monitoring	1. The financial group tends to analyze sampled data while the non-financial group tends to analyze all data.

by the following reasons:

(1)   Typically, minicomputer installations tend to have less formal computer capacity planning functions.   For example, prediction of resource requirements may not be done on a regular basis in these installations.   This reason accounts for the two mainframe groups' more frequent reliance on formal prediction of future scenarios (utilization for CPU, storage requirements and data access for disk) in making equipment upgrade decisions.   Note that Table 5.3 indicates statistically significant results in Questions 2a, 3a and 3b.

(2)   Minicomputer installations tend to serve users with special needs which may require certain computer service performance levels. This explains the mini group's more frequent use of discussions with users in setting performance objectives in comparison with the mainframe groups.

(3)   Most commercially developed software facilities are targeted for IBM and IBM compatible systems due to their large market base.   Performance modeling packages, system monitoring packages, and statistical packages allowing for workload forecasting, are no exceptions.   This explains the more frequent use of performance modeling packages for response time prediction, the more use of time-series regression techniques for workload projection, the more use of measures with breakdowns by workload types by the IBM group, and the tendency that the IBM group collects data continuously while the non-IBM group collects sampled data only.

5.4.2 Computer Budget

Availability of resources and expertise is an important cause for the differences between the large and the small budget groups in their capacity planning practices. For example, the prediction of technological innovation is practiced significantly more often by the large budget group. Such a prediction in general requires thorough and broad (industry-wide) understanding of what is available today, what is under research and development, and what user requirements are most demanded. Not every data processing department is willing to allocate resources for the task of technological forecasts. The large budget group also rated the use of analytical techniques for predicting response time much higher than the small budget group. Again not every installation will feel the need to use these methods which require a large upfront cost to set up and implement. When the operation is sufficiently large, relying only on judgmental methods will become infeasible. To perform effective analysis one must have a good understanding of the interrelated behavior of the system. The system modeling approach reinforces this concept. The use of this approach requires a good knowledge of the internal working of the system which is affected by many factors including, for example, scheduling policies which can give a significant effect on system performances [Horvath, Lam and Sethi 1977]. Due to the economics of scale, the allocation of resources to apply sophisticated quantitative techniques in an attempt to achieve more accurate predictions becomes justifiable in large installations.

The same line of logic applies to the large budget group's sig-

nificantly more frequent performance of extensive analysis of the effect
of response time on user productivity in setting response time
objectives, and their more frequent use of the various techniques for
workload projections. In order to use many of these quantitative
techniques, workload measures other than the total CPU hours consumed
are needed. For example, transaction/job counts are needed in many
queueing models, and network traffic load is needed in order to estimate
the amount of network delay which is part of the interactive response
time.

The tendency of collecting data more often and using more data for
analysis by the large budget group is reasonable. The more data one
collects, the more resources (human and computer) are required to store,
maintain, and manipulate the data. Large installations will be more
able to afford the necessary resources.

5.4.3 Extent of Direct Charging

User scrutiny of the cost and performance of data center leads to
the differences among the no-charge/partly-charge/fully-charge groups in
their computer capacity planning practices. As summarized in Table 5.4,
computer centers that directly charge back the cost of their services
more likely base their equipment upgrade decisions on formal prediction
of future scenarios (utilization of CPU and storage requirements of
disk) and they perform prediction of response time more often than the
non-charging group. In order to maintain or improve services in a cost-
effective manner, the charging groups would also likely monitor the

availability of new technologies to take advantage of any price/ performance breakthrough. Consequently, technological forecasts are practiced more often by the charging groups.

The charging groups also put significantly more emphasis on: setting performance objectives, the scientific analysis of the effect of response time on user productivity in setting up these objectives, and the use of performance prediction in making CPU upgrade decisions. These results are logical. When users are directly charged for the computer services, they will likely pay more attention to the services that they are receiving. Service performance will naturally become an important issue. The computer center must, therefore, watch out for how well they will be able to provide their services and plan ahead to avoid significant performance degradation.

The charging for the various computer services must be reviewed periodically (typically on an annual basis) and the rates revised according to the costs, expected workload, and the data center's intention to encourage or discourage the use of certain services. Standard full cost is a common method used to determine the charge rates [Chan and Lam 1986]. The projected workload plays an important role in this method. A close relationship between the projected workload and the actual workload means that the costs can be fully or almost fully recovered from charging, an important objective of a charging system. It is therefore conceivable that the charging groups place more emphasis on workload forecasts. This expectation is confirmed by the survey results which show the charging groups project workload more often than the non-charging group using trending, regression and user surveys. The use of more sophisticated methods does not exhibit any significant difference, however.

Charging, when done in sufficient details, would normally require most resources to be accounted for. This explains the more frequent use of the many different workload measures by the charging groups, and their use of more detailed system monitoring data.

5.4.4 Industry Characteristics - Financial versus Non-Financial

The special requirements of the computer users in financial institutions result in significant differences from the non-financial counterpart in their practices for capacity planning as summarized in Table 5.4. The financial group consists of banks, insurance companies, and other financial organizations such as investment houses, savings and loan associations, etc. Computer systems in these organizations typically consist of a large communication network. The computer users at the terminals are often waiting for response from the system in order to service the clients. Therefore, interactive response time is important and directly affects the organizations' ability to conduct business. This characteristic is reflected in the significantly higher ratings given by the financial group to the use of predicted response time in the decisions for their CPU upgrades. They also emphasize more on performance objectives.

The financial group's use of the various approaches for predicting response time, and the use of network traffic as workload measure are also significantly more than the non-financial group, confirming again their emphasis on interactive response time. The real time processing requirement of some major transactions, e.g, account withdrawals and updates, may explain their more frequent practice of predicting innova- tion on disk technology for their decisions on disk upgrades.

The financial group is found to use sample data for computer capacity planning analysis more often than the non-financial group. This is likely due to the large computer networks associated with the financial institutions. Analysis of data for large networks often in- volves a great deal of processing. Sampling is therefore particulaly cost effective in this circumstance.

5.5   Other Environmental Factors

The remaining five factors analyzed turned out to have less effect than the four factors in Table 5.4 on the practices of capacity planning. For example, we had expected that the High Tech industry to be a leader in the use of advanced techniques for computer capacity planning. This expectation, however, turned out to be unsupported. From our test results, non-high tech companies, as a whole, view com- puter capacity planning just as important a function as high tech com- panies and are just as ready to use any available tools and techniques as they see fit. The comparison between the Industrial and Service groups of respondents shows little difference in their capacity planning practices. This confirms our belief that because of the diverse lines of business within each group averaging out the effects of each other,

their needs in user computing as a group show no significant difference
in the capacity planning functions.   Each individual industry has its
own combination of environmental characteristics which result in significant differences in some aspects of its computer capacity planning
practices as evidenced in the average ratings of selected questions.
For the interest of readers involved in specific industries, average
ratings for those industries with ten or more respondents according to
Table 4.1 are shown in Table 5.5.

The extent of interactive and database usage had been selected as
two of the environmental variables in this study because both the interactive and database services have the effect of bringing computers
closer to the user.   Computer system performance is therefore a more
visible issue among organizations with high interactive and database
usage.   As visibility increases, a greater effort may need to be spent
on computer capacity planning.   Furthermore, with database systems, the
adequacy of online storage becomes a major concern.   Therefore, the percentage of interactive usage and database usage were expected to have an
impact on the capacity planning practices.

Our data show that these two factors have influence on some, though
not all, aspects of capacity planning practices among the respondents.
For example, installations with heavy interactive usage did show significantly heavier use of network traffic as the workload measure.   And
for establishing performance objectives, the approach based on extensive
analysis of the effect of response time on user productivity is used
significantly more often by the heavy database usage group.

Our analysis based on the amount of computer utilization for the capacity planning function did not yield statistically significant results probably due to the extreme distribution--87% of the respondents belong to one utilization group (i.e., 5% or less of total workload spent on data collection and analysis for computer capacity planning).

The four environmental factors were expected to be correlated. A multiple analysis of variance was used to investigate the possible interaction effects among them. The results show that variations in the respondents' ratings are largely explained by individual main-effect factors, and that the interaction effects in most cases are not significant.

5.6 Further Implications

The results as presented in this chapter indicate that there are indeed differences in the practice of computer capacity planning under different circumstances. Four major environmental factors have been identified: computer facility, computer budget, the extent of direct charging, and the financial versus non-financial industry characteristics. Further implications of these results include:

(1) Predicting interactive response time as a part of the process in the decision making for disk upgrade is not done very frequently. This is a clear evidence that the component approach is still largely predominant in computer capacity planning practices.

TABLE 5.5

MEAN RATINGS BY INDUSTRY

Definition of ratings: 1 = frequently used   2 = sometimes used
                       3 = occasionally used 4 = rarely/never used

---

Questions in Questionnaire Relating to Computer Capacity Planning
Practices

---

2. Methods used to determine when CPU upgrade is required
   a) Predict CPU utilization
   b) Predict performance eg. response time
   c) Predict technological innovations

3. Methods used to determine when disk upgrade is required
   a) Predict disk storage requirements
   b) Predict data access rate
   c) Predict response time
   d) Predict technological innovations
   e) Acquire new disk along with new CPU

4. Methods used to predict response time
   a) Plot and extrapolate
   b) Use simple queueing models
   c) Use queueing network models
   d) Use performance modeling packages
   e) Use synthetic load benchmarking

5. Methods used to establish performance objectives
   a) Based on past performance experiences
   b) Based on industry-wide practice
   c) Based on negotiations with major user groups
   d) Based on extensive analysis of the effect of response time on
      user productivity

6. Methods used for projecting computer workload
   a) Visual trending
   b) Use time-series regression
   c) Use structural models
   d) Use sophisticated forecasting techniques
   e) Survey users for their own projections

7. Measurement of workload
   a) Total CPU hours consumed
   b) CPU hours consumed by workload class
   c) Transaction/job counts
   d) Total composite measure units (e.g. service units on IBM
      systems)
   e) Composite measure units by workload class
   f) Traffic rate in communication network

8. Data collection and analysis practice
   a) Collect continuously and analyze all data
   b) Collect continuously and analyze sample data
   c) Collect and use sample data
   d) Collect only as required at irregular intervals

TABLE 5.5 (Cont'd)

Mean Ratings by Industry

	4* Chem*	5 Elec	6 Food	16 Paper	17 Petro	24 Bank	25 Fin	26 Life	27 Retai	28 Serv	29 Trans	30 Util
2.												
a	1.56	1.44	1.83	1.17	1.31	1.33	1.60	1.50	1.40	1.80	1.50	1.41
b	2.00	1.56	2.39	1.33	2.25	1.57	1.69	1.66	1.93	1.83	1.80	1.79
c	2.56	3.00	2.83	3.17	2.75	2.43	2.71	2.53	2.93	2.73	2.70	2.68
3.												
a	1.39	1.39	1.33	1.42	1.13	1.39	1.26	1.22	1.93	1.50	1.10	1.32
b	2.94	2.94	3.22	2.25	2.81	2.57	2.63	2.63	2.87	3.03	2.40	3.12
c	2.33	1.83	2.72	2.67	2.38	2.33	2.31	2.06	2.47	2.48	1.90	2.35
d	3.22	3.17	2.72	3.33	2.63	2.52	2.83	2.34	3.27	2.93	2.90	2.71
e	3.11	3.22	2.83	3.25	3.31	2.70	3.26	3.09	3.20	2.95	3.00	3.26
4.												
a	2.56	2.41	1.80	2.18	2.44	1.82	2.00	2.07	2.54	2.42	2.60	2.52
b	2.22	2.82	3.07	2.73	3.25	2.43	2.52	2.66	2.62	3.00	2.70	3.25
c	3.45	3.59	3.46	3.55	3.19	2.82	3.03	3.17	3.38	3.47	3.00	3.36
d	3.67	3.17	3.33	3.64	2.69	2.46	2.71	2.33	2.46	2.75	3.30	2.82
e	3.50	3.18	3.20	3.91	3.56	3.23	3.20	3.63	3.38	3.20	2.60	3.46
5.												
a	1.67	1.62	1.69	1.80	1.54	1.68	1.72	1.46	1.77	1.58	1.78	1.78
b	2.93	3.12	3.31	3.50	2.54	2.88	2.91	2.97	3.23	2.96	2.89	2.78
c	2.54	1.94	2.46	2.50	1.93	1.90	1.88	2.10	2.23	2.15	2.00	1.97
d	3.33	2.37	3.16	2.80	2.77	2.58	2.72	3.00	2.77	2.86	2.22	3.19
6.												
a	1.72	1.67	1.72	1.25	1.75	1.78	1.74	2.03	2.00	1.85	1.90	2.18
b	2.61	2.61	3.00	3.17	2.75	2.70	2.91	2.56	3.33	3.25	2.80	1.94
c	2.83	2.22	2.44	2.58	2.44	2.11	2.09	2.25	2.13	2.38	1.90	2.82
d	3.78	3.61	3.83	3.75	3.75	3.48	3.77	3.75	4.00	3.80	3.50	3.56
e	2.67	2.33	2.33	2.75	1.69	2.00	2.54	2.28	2.53	2.45	1.90	2.06
7.												
a	2.11	1.61	1.78	2.17	1.75	1.78	1.97	2.47	2.00	1.90	2.40	1.68
b	2.00	1.56	1.72	2.33	1.69	1.70	1.69	1.84	1.67	2.03	2.00	1.59
c	2.06	1.94	1.94	1.83	2.06	1.89	1.63	1.66	1.80	2.08	1.60	1.79
d	2.33	2.56	2.94	3.25	2.81	2.46	2.74	2.44	3.00	2.78	2.40	2.82
e	2.67	2.89	3.22	2.91	2.63	2.43	2.97	2.41	2.93	2.95	2.40	2.94
f	2.67	2.22	2.67	2.75	2.75	1.93	1.83	2.09	2.47	2.43	1.80	2.74
8.												
a	2.50	2.56	1.72	2.08	2.56	2.33	3.14	2.53	2.40	2.45	2.40	1.79
b	2.89	2.61	2.61	2.33	2.44	2.09	2.23	2.63	2.20	2.65	2.60	2.35
c	2.94	2.17	2.83	2.58	2.56	2.48	2.20	2.47	2.47	2.63	2.50	2.85
d	3.11	2.83	3.39	3.50	3.13	3.17	3.06	2.94	3.33	2.63	2.50	3.35

*   The numbering for industries corresponds to that in Table 4.1 and
the industry names are abbreviated in this table heading.

(2) As expected, the IBM group does use performance modeling packages more often than the other groups. This is mainly due to the availability of modeling software packages for the large population of IBM and IBM compatible installations. This implies that the development of performance modeling packages for non-IBM equipment can be a fruitful and welcome endeavor.

(3) Extensive analysis of the effect of response time on user productivity are conducted significantly more often by the large budget group and the charging group. Such analysis are not high priority items for the management when the operations of an installation are not large, or user scrutiny on cost and benefits of computer services is not present. Those organizations which have small computer operations or do not charge back their computer services will stand to gain if industry-wide data on performance objectives can be made more readily available.

(4) Even though visual trending is the predominant method for computer workload forecasting, our comparison results show that large budget installations do attempt to use all the other techniques listed in the questionnaire much more often than the small budget group. This seems to imply that large installations feel the need for better methods for workload forecasting. Indeed workload projection is the cornerstone of computer capacity planning. An inaccurate forecast will invalidate any fine analysis thus will likely result in poor planning and financial loss. Currently, workload forecasting is the weakest element in the entire capacity planning process. More study is warranted in this area.

(5) The comparison results show that the total CPU-hour consumption is used as a measure of computer workload about equally often

across all the groups analyzed. However, the large budget group and the charging group have used other listed measures more often than the small budget group and the non-charging group, respectively. This indicates the inadequacy of the total CPU-hour consumption as computer workload measure.

(6) Predicting performance for upgrade decisions and using scientific methods for performance predictions are practiced more frequently by the large budget group than the small budget group. This confirms that time, effort, and expertise are the major considerations for these practices. The system modeling approach is therefore more applicable to large installations, at least with the current technology.

5.7 Summary

A wide variety of tools and techniques exist for the various aspects of computer capacity planning. These tools and techniques differ in their underlying assumptions, the degree of difficulty to understand, the amount of time and effort to implement, the volume of data required to collect and analyze, and the insight they can provide on the system behavior (present and future). Not all techniques are appropriate for every installation. A capacity planner should select the methodology that is most suitable for the environment of his or her organization.

Four environmental variables have been identified to be particularly significant in affecting capacity planning practices. These

are the computer facility, computer budget, the extent of direct
charging, and the financial versus non-financial industry
characteristics. Their specific effects and the profile of the respondents as reported in this chapter provide a useful reference for computer capacity planners in carrying out the planning functions in their
own computing and business environment. Researchers should also find
this information useful for developing and refining capacity planning
tools taking relevant environmental factors into consideration. As indicated from the responses to our survey, different tools and techniques
exhibit different degree of usefulness under different computing and
business environments. This kind of direct consumer information should
serve as useful guidelines for equipment manufacturers and software
developers in the design of their future products.

CHAPTER 6

SUMMARY AND RECOMMENDATIONS

6.1 A Review

Computer capacity planning refers to the process of monitoring and projecting computer workload and planning for the change or expansion of computer configurations to satisfy future demands in a cost-effective manner. Due to the large amount of resources involved in most major equipment acquisitions, even a small improvement in the capacity planning process can result in significant cost savings. With the appearance of publications and other activities on the subject, computer capacity planning has emerged from the business folklore. While much of the literature has concentrated on explaining the principles and techniques that can be used for computer capacity planning, not much work has been done to assess the extent these principles and techniques have been applied in practice. What is happening in practice is of interest to practicing capacity planners, researchers, equipment manufacturers, software developers as well as auditors who are in the position of providing management advisory services in regards to the efficiency of

195

corporate operations.

In the previous chapters we have summarized and assessed the approaches and methods available for computer capacity planning as well as
a research study to investigate the applicability of these approaches
and methods based on a questionnaire survey. In the next section, we
will provide a summary comparison between theory and practices, that is,
the methodologies available in literature versus what is being practiced
in reality. Section 6.3 discusses some recommendations on measures that
may help bring theory and practice closer together to improve the
quality of the capacity planning process, which in turn contributes to
cost savings. Areas that require further research are also identified
and discussed.

6.2 A Summary Comparison Between Theory and Practice

A successful data center relies on a cost-effective capacity planning program that can ensure sufficient computer capacity to provide
satisfactory services to its users. The previous chapters have outlined
the methodologies available for implementing these tasks, and the extent
these methods are used in practice as evidenced from the results of our
questionnaire survey of the Fortune companies. From the survey results,
it is apparent that many of the available techniques have not been fil-
tered through to become common practice, and that several environmental
factors have important influence on the application of these techniques.
More specifically, when comparing theory with practices, the following

areas of particular interest to both practitioners and researchers have been identified:

(1)   In conducting computer capacity planning studies to identify the need for configuration change or capacity upgrade, the component approach is widely in use despite the rapid development of the system modeling methodology and the availability of performance modeling software packages.

(2)   Performance objectives are established mostly based on the installation's past performance experiences.   There have been a great amount of literature dealing with the impact of computer performance (especially terminal response time and its degree of variation) on user productivity, and a number of studies showing that different types of work call for different performance requirements. However, in practice, analysis of the effect of performance on user productivity is not conducted very often for the purpose of establishing performance objectives.   The process of negotiations with major users seems to be gaining momentum, but is still not as widely used as past performance experiences.

(3)   Workload forecasting is done mostly based on visual trending despite the existence of the many sophisticated forecasting methods discussed in the literature.

(4)   Short of an ideal workload measure, CPU-hour consumption and transaction/job counts are widely used as the measures of computer workload. Composite measure units such as service units on IBM systems and standard units of processing on UNIVAC systems are not in common

use.

(5)   From the way that data collection and analysis are practiced, it is evident that the majority of the organizations are treating computer capacity planning as an on-going process.   There is still a small percentage (11% of the respondents) of the organizations does it on an ad hoc basis.   Sampling is used quite often for the analysis of workload and performance data, reflecting the concern of efficiency in carrying out the computer capacity planning functions.   Theory appears to be falling behind in this aspect, in that not much theory has been established dealing with the proper use of different sampling techniques for the analysis of system data for the purpose of computer capacity planning.

(6)   Several environmental factors have been found to have significant effect on the practice of the various aspects of computer capacity planning.   This implies that the gap between theory and practice for specific aspects of capacity planning is wider in some segments of the industry than others.   For example, installations that directly charge back users for their computer services tend to employ the more advanced techniques for identifying the need for upgrade, for workload forecasting and for establishing performance objectives.   IBM and IBM compatible installations use performance modeling packages more often than non-IBM installations.   Financial institutions measure network traffic rate as the workload indicator more often than their non-financial counterparts, reflecting their heavy emphasis on computer communications networks.

6.3   Recommendations

A capacity planner should always look for ways to enhance the planning process.   We hope this study provide some guidances in this
respect.   To improve the theory and practice of capacity planning, some
of the more important measures include the following :

Continuing Education
Continuing education on the up-to-date development of capacity
planning methodologies should be useful for capacity planners.   These
courses should emphasize the fundamental concepts and rationale underlying the methods.   A cookbook style, how-to-do-it course that does not
provide an understanding of the theory will not allow a capacity planner
to grow, therefore will be ineffective in the long run.   Not all
capacity planning approaches and methodologies are applicable to every
environment.   Knowing what methods are available and the underlying assumptions and rationale of each method will facilitate a capacity planner to make the right choice for the required analysis in each study.
Due to the amount involved in major equipment acquisitions, the savings
from a more reliable analysis can be substantial.   Therefore, such a
continuing education program for capacity planners should prove to be a
worthwhile investment for most organizations.

Software Packages and Input Data
The survey results indicate that IBM and IBM compatible installations use performance modeling packages more often than others to pre-

dict computer performance. More performance modeling packages should be developed for non-IBM systems to encourage the use of modeling. The availability of a software package, however, does not necessarily guarantee its proper use. Training for the use of these packages must emphasize on the rationale underlying the methods used in the software. The preparation of model input data was often cited as a major difficulty in the use of the modeling software. Some effort to ease this problem was made by BGS's introduction of a separate software product called Capture/MVS which automatically extracts the required input parameters for BEST/1 from the software and accounting monitor data on the IBM MVS systems [BGS 1982]. Similar products should be developed for other modeling packages on other computer systems.

Functional Organization

Currently most installations organize their computer capacity planning function along the hardware components. For example, a typical configuration planning and support department may consist of a planning section and a performance section. The planning section typically is responsible for CPU capacity upgrades, and the performance section is responsible for the monitoring and reporting of the computer performance. Under this organization, capacity planning often means the planning of CPU upgrades. The upgrades for all other components falls into the category of performance tuning, therefore are the responsibilities of the performance section. For example, if the monitored data indicate excessive paging activities, then an addition of memory may be called for in order to reduce paging delay. The monitoring and "tuning" of the various components on the system are usually handled by subunits of the performance section. Typically performance section may have a subunit for the disk system, another subunit for the communications network, and so on. Such an organization naturally leads to the component approach for capacity planning.

To apply the system modeling approach and to encourage the use of more advanced techniques where applicable, an organization by function will be more appropriate. With this organization, a configuration planning and support department may consist of a workload measurement and forecasting section, a performance monitoring and tuning section, and a performance prediction and capacity revision section. Each section deals with a particular aspect of planning for the entire computer system: the workload, the performance monitoring and improvment of the existing system, and the planning of a new configuration to meet future requirements. Each section will choose the approaches and methods most suitable for the nature of the tasks to be done. This organization has the advantage of pooling staff with expertise in a particular function into one unit, thus should encourage more advanced methodologies to be employed.

Cost-effectiveness of Capacity Planning and Case Studies

One serious concern in many organizations is the cost of carrying out the capacity planning function. Capacity planners are responsible for selecting the most cost-effective methodology in a given situation and environment. A prerequisite for this to be possible is the capacity planner's familiarity with the various modern methods. Continuing education for capacity planners as mentioned earlier is important here. To further help make an intelligent choice, researchers can carry out and report case studies that compare the accuracy and efficiency of different methods. For instance, comparisons may be made between visual trending and regression for workload forecasting, the component approach and the system modeling aproach for upgrade timing prediction, and so forth. Efficiency of a method can be measured in terms of machine resources (processing and data storage) as well as human resources. With more case studies of this kind, more organizations will be able to justify the use of new methods that can be more cost-effective to them but was not previously attempted due to concerns over cost.

Improvement in Workload Forecasts

Workload forecasting is the weakest element in the process of computer capacity planning. Many capacity planners may very well realize the potential advantage of the more sophisticated system analysis techniques such as queueing network medeling, but have opted not to use them. Their rationale is that, when the projected workload is only a crude estimate, the improvement on accuracy by using a more sophisticated system analysis method is very doubtful. It is clear that workload forecasting must be improved if the theory and practice of computer capacity planning are to be advanced. Research on computer workload forecasting must take into consideration the special characteristics of computer workload data such as latent demand, peak-to-average ratio, seasonal and cyclical pattern, influence on workload increase due to the trend of increasing size and sophistication of software packages, relationship between computer workload and business volume, corporate plans as well as major user departments' decisions related to their computer use. One beneficial study, for example, would be to examine the relevent types of information that can be provided by the corporate planning office and user departments for the improvment in workload forecasts. In the area of system analysis, studies should include the effect on the accuracy of the various analytical techniques such as queueing network modeling under different degrees of workload forecast uncertainty.

User Productivity Studies

Most computer facilities are installed to enhance user productivity. With the continuing rise of labor cost and the increasing access to computers through terminals, the effect of terminal response time on user productivity has become an important issue. This effect is of interest to computer capacity planners since it should be a major consideration in establishing response time objectives. It is generally recognized that different types of work to be performed at the computer terminal will be affected differently by varying the response time. Some experiments have been reported giving the specific effects for the types of work studied, including the task completion rate, error rate, and user satisfaction. These experiments have helped clarify some issues, but substantial effort remains before a predictive model can emerge. Currently, not many organizations conduct analysis of the effect of response time on user productivity, according to our survey results. In many installations such an analysis may not be feasible due to cost, lack of control mechanism to vary response times, inadequate user cooperation, etc. To make other's experimental results useful for capacity planners, some kind of classification scheme must be devised to allow the characterization of the different types of terminal work. The effect of response time on user productivity can then be correlated to the terminal work characteristics.

Research on Sampling Techniques for Capacity Planning

Sampling appears to be commonly used in practice, especially for data analysis. Theoretical foundations on the application of sampling techniques for computer capacity planning await development, however. Many questions need to be answered in this aspect of research. Which sampling techniques are most appropriate for data collection of different components (CPU, disks, network, etc.)? Which are appropriate for data analysis? What are the expected errors? What are the trade-offs between efficiency and accuracy? Do the computer workload and performance data exhibit any special characteristics that can exploit certain special sampling techniques? Do the business and computing environments have any effect on these characteristics? Answers to these and other questions will have significant contributions to better measurement, which in turn will help improve workload and performance prediction. Consequently better capacity plans can be derived to achieve greater cost savings.

<u>Exchange Programs</u>

More exchange programs should be established between academia and business organizations in order to narrow the gap between theory and practice. Such exchange programs can take the form of faculty on leave to work in business organizations, or practitioners in residence to work in academic institutions. These programs should on the one hand help speed up the filtering of existing methods available in literature to real world applications, and on the other hand provide academic researchers with the opportunity to better understand practical problems, thereby enhancing the practical significance of their future research.

REFERENCES

ACM Computing Surveys (various authors), Special Issue: Queueing Network Models of Computer System Performance (September 1978).

Allen, Arnold O., Probability, Statistics, and Queueing Theory with Computer Science Applications (New York: Academic Press, 1978).

Anderberg, M.R., Cluster Analysis for Applications (New York: Academic Press, 1973).

Anderson, Gordon E., "The Coordinated Use of Five Performance Evaluation Methodologies," Communications ACM (February 1984), pp. 119-125.

Artis, H.P., "Forecasting Computer Requirements: An Analyst's Dilemma," EDP Performance Review (February 1980) pp. 1-5.

Axelrod, C. Warren, Computer Productivity - A Planning Guide for Cost-Effective Management (New York: John Wiley and Sons, 1982).

Barber, R.E. and H.C. Lucas, Jr., "System Response Time Operator Productivity, and Job Satisfaction," Communications ACM (November 1983), pp. 972-986.

Barkataki, Shan, "A CPE Project in a Fast Transaction Processing Environment," CMG Proceedings (1984), pp. 9-14.

Baskett, F., K.M. Chandy, R.R. Muntz, and F. Palacios-Gomez, "Open, Closed, and Mixed Networks of Queues with Different Classes of Customers," Journal of ACM (April 1975), pp. 248-260.

BGS Systems, Inc., Best/1 User's Guide (Waltham, MA, 1982).

Biasi, Orazio, "Workload Forecasting Methodology," Proceedings IIM (April 1985), pp. 211-233.

Borovits, Israel, Management of Computer Operations (Englewood Cliffs, N.J.: Prentice-Hall, 1984).

Box, George and G. Jenkins, Time Series Analysis: Forecasting and Control, Revised Edition (San Francisco: Holden Day, 1976).

207

Bronner, L., "Overview of the Capacity Planning Process for Production Data Processing," IBM Systems Journal (Vol. 19, No. 1, 1980) pp. 4-27.

Brown, Robert, Smoothing, Forecasting and Prediction, (Englewood Cliffs, N.J.: Prentice-Hall, 1963).

Brumfield, J.A., "Operational Response-Time Formulas and Their Sensitivity to Error," Computer Performance (March 1984), pp. 7-13.

Burton, Kathleen, "DP Forecasters Often Still in Dark Despite CPE Tools," ComputerWorld (December 17, 1984), p. 13.

Buzen, J.P., "Computational Algorithms for Closed Queueing Networks with Exponential Servers," Communications ACM (September 1973), pp. 527-531.

Buzen, J.P., "Four Techniques for Performance Calculation," ICCCM Proceedings (1980), pp. 217-221.

Chambers, John, S. Mullick and Donald Smith, "How to Choose the Right Forecasting Technique," Harvard Business Review, (July-August 1971), pp. 45-74.

Chan, K. Hung and K. Ho, "Forecasting of Seasonal and Cyclical Financial Variables: The Wiener-Kolmogorov Method VS. the Box-Jenkins Method," Advances in Financial Planning and Forecasting (1986, forthcoming).

Chan, K. Hung and Shui F. Lam, "Transfer Pricing for Computer Services in Public Utilities," Journal of Systems Management (July 1986), pp. 23-29.

Chandy, K.M. and D. Neuse, "Linearizer: A Heuristic Algorithm for Queueing Network Models of Computing Systems," Communications ACM (February 1982), pp. 126-134.

Cochran, William, Sampling Techniques (New York: John Wiley and Sons, 1963).

Coffman, E.G., Jr., and L. Kleinrock, "Feedback Queueing Models for Time-Shared Systems," Journal of ACM (October 1968), pp. 549-576.

Coffman, E.G., Jr., R.R. Muntz and H. Trotter, "Waiting Time Distribution for Processor-Sharing Systems," Journal of ACM (January 1970), pp. 123-130.

Cortada, James, Managing DP Hardware - Capacity Planning, Cost Justification, Availability, and Energy Management (Englewood Cliffs, N.J. : Prentice-Hall, 1983).

Courtois, P.J., Decomposability: Queueing and Computer System Applications (New York: Academic Press, 1977).

Denning, P.J. and J.P. Buzen, "The Operational Analysis of Queueing Network Models," Computing Surveys (September 1978), pp. 225-261.

Emrick, R., "Capacity Management of End-User Processing," Computer Performance (June 1984), pp. 80-84.

Ferrari, D., G. Serazzi and A. Zeigner, Measurement and Tuning of Computer Systems (Englewood Cliffs, N.J.: Prentice-Hall, 1983).

Ferrari, D. and M. Spadoni (ed.) Experimental Computer Performance Evaluation (New York: North-Holland, 1981)

The Fortune 500 and the Fortune Service 500 (1984 Directory of U.S. Corporations).

The Fortune 500 and the Fortune Service 500 (1985 Directory of U.S. Corporations).

The Fortune 500 and the Fortune Service 500 (1986 Directory of U.S. Corporations).

Friedman, L'Jeanne, "Integrating Performance and Capacity Planning Considerations into the Application Design Review Process," CMG Transaction (March 1985), pp. 28-29.

Fusfeld, A.R. and R.N. Foster, "Delphi Technique: Survey and Comment," Business Horizon (March 1972), pp. 29-34.

Gill, P.E. and W. Murray (ed.) Numerical Methods for Constrained Optimization (New York: Academic Press, 1974).

Gordon, G., System Simulation, 2nd edition (Englewood Cliffs, N.J.: Prentice-Hall, 1978).

Gordon, W.J. and G.F. Newell, "Closed Queueing Systems with Exponential Servers," Operations Research (April 1967), pp. 254-265.

Groff, Gene, "Empirical Comparison of Models for Short Range Forecasting," Management Science (September 1973), pp. 23-34.

Hellerman, H. and T. Conroy, Computer System Performance (New York: McGraw Hill, 1975).

Henkel, T., "Hardware Roundup," ComputerWorld (August 8, 1983), pp.29-39.

Horvath, E., Shui F. Lam and R. Sethi, "A Level Algorithm for Preemptive Scheduling," Journal of ACM (January 1977), pp. 32-43.

IBM Corporation, OS/VS2 MVS System Programming Library: System Management Facilities (SMF), GC28-0706 (July 1977).

Information Research Associates, <u>PAWS/A User Guide</u> (Austin, TX, 1983).

Jalswal, N.K., Performance Evaluation Studies for Time-Sharing Computer Systems, <u>Performance Evaluation</u> (December 1983), pp.223-236.

Jensen, Robert, "Fantasyland Accounting Research: Let's pretend ...," <u>The Accounting Review</u> (January 1979), pp. 189-196.

Joreskog, K. and D. Sorbom, <u>LISREL, Linear Structural Relationships by the Method of Maximum Likelihood, User's Guide V</u> (National Educational Resources Inc., 1981).

Kelly, J.C., <u>Capacity Planning: A State of the Art Survey</u> (National Technical Information Services, PB83-252924, 1983).

Kendall, D.G., "Stochastic Processes Occurring in the Theory of Queues and Their Analysis by the Method of the Imbedded Markov Chain," <u>Annals of Mathematical Statistics</u> (September 1953) pp.338-354.

King, W. R., "Strategic Planning for Management Information Systems," <u>MIS Quarterly</u> (March 1978), pp.27-37.

Kleinrock, Leonard, <u>Queueing Systems, Volume I: Theory</u> (New York: John Wiley & Sons, 1975).

Kleinrock, Leonard, <u>Queueing Systems, Volume II: Computer Applications</u> (New York: John Wiley & Sons, 1976).

Lavenberg, Stephen (ed.) <u>Computer Performance Modeling Handbook</u> (New York: Academic Press, 1983).

Law, A.M. and W.D. Kelton, <u>Simulation Modeling and Analysis</u> (New York: McGraw-Hill, 1981)

Lazowska, E.D., J. Zahorjan, G.S. Graham, and K.C. Sevcik, <u>Quantitative System Performance, Computer System Analysis Using Queueing Network Models</u> (Englewood Cliffs, N.J.: Prentice-Hall, 1984).

Lewis, B.C. and A.E. Crews, "The Evolution of Benchmarking as a Computer Performance Evaluation Technique," <u>MIS Quarterly</u> (March 1985), pp. 7-16.

Linstone, Harold, and M. Turoff (ed.) <u>The Delphi Method: Techniques and Applications</u> (Reading, MA: Addison-Wesley, 1975).

Lipsky, L. and J.D. Church, "Applications of a Queueing Network Model for a Computer System," <u>Computing Surveys</u> (September 1977), pp. 205-222.

Lo, T.L., "Computer Capacity Planning Using Queueing Network Models," <u>Proceedings of IFIP W.G.7.3 International Symposium on Computer Performance Modeling, Measurement and Evaluation</u> (1980) pp. 145-152.

Luistro, F.M., "The Cone Theory as Applied to Computer Workload Forecasting" CMG Proceedings (1983) pp. 398-402.

Lyman, H.T., J. Anderson and J. Plewer, "Are You Rushing Too Fast to Subsecond Response Time?" ComputerWorld: In Depth (September 9, 1985), pp. 5-14.

Makridakis, S., A. Hodgswon and S. Wheelwright, "An Interactive Forecasting System," The American Statistician (November 1974), pp. 153-158.

Mendenhall, W. and J. Reinmuth, Statistics for Management and Economics, 2nd Edition (North Scituate, MA: Duxbury Press, 1974).

Miller, L.H., An Investigation of the Effects of Output Variability and Output Bandwidth on User Performance in an Interactive Computer System (University of Southern California Information Sciences Institute, ISI/RR-76-50, 1976).

Morino Associates, Inc., MVS Performance Management and Capacity Planning Survey Report (Morino Associates, 1983).

Morris, M. and P. Roth, Computer Performance Evaluation: Tools and Techniques for Effective Analysis (New York: Van Nostrand Reinhold, 1982).

Muntz, R.R., "Queuing Networks: A Critique of the State of the Art and Directions for the Future," Computing Surveys (September 1978), pp. 353-359.

Nelson, Charles, Applied Time Series Analysis for Managerial Forecasting (San Francisco: Holden Day, 1973).

Oppenheim, A.N., Questionnaire Design and Attitude Measurement (Basic Books, 1966).

Pick, James B., Computer Systems in Business: An Introduction (Boston, MA: PWS Publishers, 1986).

Quantitative System Performance, Inc., MAP User Guide (Seattle, WA, 1982).

Sanguinetti, J. and R. Billington, "A Multi-Class Queueing Network Model of an Interactive System," Proceedings of the CMG XI International Conference (1980), pp. 50-55.

Sarna, D.E.Y., "Forecasting Computer Resource Utilization Using Key Volume Indicators," AFIPS Conference Proceedings (1979), pp. 185-192.

SAS Institute Inc., SAS User's Guide: Statistics Version 5 Edition (Cary, North Carolina, 1985).

Sauer, C.H. and K.M. Chandy, "Approximate Solution of Queueing Models,"

Computer Magazine (April 1980), pp. 25-32.

Sauer, C.H. and K.M. Chandy, Computer Systems Performance Modeling (Englewood Cliffs, N.J.: Prentice-Hall, 1981).

Sauer, C.H. and E. A. MacNair, "The Research Queueing Package: Past, Present and Future," Proceedings of the National Computer Conference AFEPS (1982), Arlington, Virginia.

Schaeffer, Howard, Data Center Operations: A Guide to Effective Planning, Processing, and Performance (Englewood Cliffs, N.J.: Prentice-Hall, 1981)

Schindler, Paul, Jr., "End User Computing Hinders Capacity Planners," Information Systems News (September 10, 1984), p. 29.

Shneiderman, B., "Response Time and Display Rate in Human Performance with Computers," Computing Surveys (September 1984), pp. 265-285.

Smith, Dick, "A Business Case for Subsecond Response Time: Faster Is Better," ComputerWorld: In Depth (April 18, 1983), pp. 1-7.

SPSS Inc., SPSSX User's Guide 2nd ed. (1986).

Stamps, D., "DASD: Too Much Ain't Enough," Datamation (December 15, 1985), pp. 22-26.

Strauss, Melvin J., Computer Capacity: A Production Control Approach (New York: Van Nostrand Reinhold, 1981)

Stroebel, G.J., R.D. Baxter, and M.J. Denning, "A Capacity Planning Expert System for IBM System/38," Computer (July 1986), pp. 42-50.

Thadhani, A.J., "Interactive User Productivity," IBM Systems Journal (Vol. 20, No. 4, 1981), pp. 407-423.

Umbaugh, R.E., DP Resource Planning (Auerbach Publishers, May-June 1982).

Verity, J.W., "1986 DP Budget Survey," Datamation (March 15, 1985), pp. 74-78.

Wandzilak, John, "Problems Facing Workload Forecasting," CMG Proceedings (1984), pp. 506-509.

Williams, J.D. and J.S. Swenson, "Functional Workload Characteristics and Computer Response Time in the Design of On-Line Systems," Proceedings of the 13th Computer Performance Evaluation Users Group Meeting (October 1977), pp. 3-11.

Zachman, J. A., "Business Systems Planning and Business Information Control Study: A Comparison," IBM Systems Journal (No. 1, 1982) pp. 31-53.